THE BATTLE
LYS 1918

NORTH: OBJECTIVE YPRES

Battleground series:

THE BATTLE OF THE
LYS 1918
NORTH: OBJECTIVE YPRES

CHRIS BAKER

Series Editor
Nigel Cave

Pen & Sword
MILITARY

First published in Great Britain in 2018 by
Pen & Sword Military
an imprint of
Pen & Sword Books Ltd
47 Church Street,
Barnsley
South Yorkshire,
S70 2AS

ISBN 978 152671 700 9

A CIP catalogue record for this book is
available from the British Library.

Typeset in Times New Roman by Chic Graphics

Printed and bound in England by
CPI Group (UK) Ltd., Croydon, CR0 4YY

Pen & Sword Books Ltd incorporates the imprints of
Pen & Sword Archaeology, Atlas, Aviation, Battleground, Discovery,
Family History, History, Maritime, Military, Naval, Politics,
Railways, Select, Social History, Transport, True Crime,
Claymore Press, Frontline Books, Leo Cooper, Praetorian Press,
Remember When, Seaforth Publishing and Wharncliffe.

For a complete list of Pen & Sword titles please contact
PEN & SWORD BOOKS LIMITED
47 Church Street, Barnsley, South Yorkshire, S70 2AS, England
E-mail: enquiries@pen-and-sword.co.uk
Website: www.pen-and-sword.co.uk

Contents

Dedication

This book is dedicated to the memory of a man who had no connection to the Battle of the Lys at all, but without whom I would never have developed an interest in military history. Frank Hubert Wilson, born in Birmingham in 1879, served in the Royal Warwickshire Regiment (Militia) in 1897 and the Royal Marine Light Infantry 1897-1901. He re-enlisted for war service in the Royal Field Artillery (Territorial) in 1915 and served until he was discharged on medical grounds after receiving a wound in 1916. Despite this, Frank was conscripted in August 1917 and once again was discharged on medical grounds in January 1918. He was my maternal grandfather, who died before I was born; yet he led me into a thirty years' search for his story, and in so doing opened my eyes to the Great War.

Introduction

April 1918: a most critical month for the British Armies in France and Flanders, when they fought against the third major German offensive that they had faced within a matter of weeks.

I find it curious that the month appears to attract little public and academic attention, despite the fact that the action took place within a short distance of Ypres and that the British force there was greatly endangered. The fighting was of a very large scale and accounted for British and Dominion casualties of around 82,000 dead, wounded and missing (large proportion of which were men taken prisoner in the rapid early German advance). It may be because this period of fighting goes by a variety of names. For the British, the fighting in Flanders was eventually given the official name of the Battles of the Lys. The title comes from the river that flows through the battlefield, and it is *battles* because the committee that agreed such things defined it as a number of phases. The French call it *La Bataille de la Lys*; the Portuguese have it as the *Batalha de la Lys*. The Germans take a wider view. They called their attack Operation Georgette, but the fighting is often referred to as the *Vierte Flandernschlacht* (Fourth Battle of Flanders), part of the *Grosse Schlacht in Frankreich* (Great Battle in France). I have even seen it called the Fourth Battle of Ypres, but I find that misleading. For ease, I call it the Battle of the Lys.

The battlefield stretches from the La Bassée Canal near Givenchy-lez-la-Bassée, northwards past Armentières and almost to the very gates of Ypres – a front line before the German attack of some thirty-seven kilometres. It can be considered as two distinct and different topographical regions, in which the landscape played an important part in the way that the fighting developed. It is a matter of convenience for the historian that the two regions align with the German command structure.

This volume, *Objective Ypres*, covers the northern region of the battlefield, which was attacked by the German *Fourth Army* from 10 April 1918 onwards. The approximate dividing line between *Objective Ypres* and the southern volume, *Objective Hazebrouck*, is the Armentières – Bailleul railway.

Introduction by the Series Editor

This is the second volume of Chris Baker's books on the Battles of the Lys 1918; when read in conjunction with Phil Tomaselli's earlier book in the series on the fighting around Givenchy, this completes *Battleground Europe*'s overall coverage of this strangely neglected German offensive.

Inevitably there is a certain amount of overlap between Chris's two books, as in each case the context of the offensive has to be provided for an understanding of operations in the northern or southern sector. However, each geographical area, although both an integral part of the offensive, has a distinct thrust: in this case the importance of the Flanders Hills and the prolonging of the offensive into the latter part of April, capped by the extraordinary German achievement of taking Kemmelberg.

This northern part of the offensive is one in which I have a particular interest. My grandfather, RQMS Arthur Cave, 7th Leicesters, kept a brief diary during the war, which he typed up some years later. His division was one of those unfortunates that was engaged in three of the German offensives – on the Somme, at the Lys and on the Aisne. In the case of the Lys he describes hard fighting near and around Bedford House.

This book takes the visitor over parts of the battlefield that are well known to many: for Messines Ridge, particularly 1914 and 1917; in the Salient proper, the war seemed to be a never-ending slog, a daily endurance test, made even more miserable by large scale actions. Of all the years of the war, I suspect that it is the events in the Salient of 1918 that are the least known. This book is an important contribution in correcting this neglect.

My grandfather's division, the 21st, was a fairly unremarkable formation. It suffered horrendous casualties in the Spring offensives, more or less losing the numerical equivalent of all its infantry in the process of stemming the German tide. Its ranks were replaced with very large numbers of young conscripts. One might have thought that it would play a minor, quiet role in the remaining months of the war, as it rebuilt and retrained. Far from it. From the latter end of August right through to the Armistice, the division was never far from a battle zone, in the process again enduring huge casualties.

What is the point of making this observation? Simply this: although the quality of the BEF's manpower may well have been significantly degraded by the end of 1917, the fact is that these young men performed extraordinarily well in 1918, especially given the circumstances. This was the result of quality in depth: by 1918 there was a substantial reservoir of talented, capable leadership, perhaps most significantly amongst the NCOs and officers at platoon, company and battalion level.

The battles of 1918 have been described as a triumph of the British Army, which it certainly was; in my opinion it is the performance of these young conscripts and of their immediate commanders that stands out, an opinion that these books go far to substantiate.

Nigel Cave
Ratcliffe College, Spring 2018

List of Maps

Chapter One

The Background to the Battle

The Great War in French Flanders
The area in which the Battle of the Lys took place is in the ancient region of Flanders, spanning areas on both sides of the Franco-Belgian border that was established when Belgium became an independent state in 1830. The region had, and in many ways retains to this day, a common cultural tradition despite the influence of two national characteristics, political and economic structures.

War came to French and Belgian West Flanders in October 1914. German forces advanced across Belgium seeking to outflank the French and British *Entente* allies on their northern side, and encountered the allies as they too advanced with the same intention. With the remnant of the Belgian army also coming into the area having evacuated besieged Antwerp, fighting developed and took place all the way along the line from the North Sea, down past Ypres and Armentières and into the industrial coalfield area of Béthune and Lens. It was in effect one, single, climactic battle but is officially recognised as, from north to south, the Battle of the Yser, the First Battle of Ypres, and the Battles of Messines, Armentières and La Bassée. By mid-November 1914 the German gambit of attacking France with the intention of rapid victory had been defeated, and the two sides had dug in.

During December 1914 the allies went onto the offensive. In Flanders, urged by French Commander-in-Chief Joffre, the British carried out a series of small-scale, piecemeal attacks that achieved nothing but long casualty lists. I have described them in *The Truce* (Amberley, 2014). Sadly, they set a pattern for years to come. Much larger attacks, at Neuve Chapelle (March 1915), Aubers and Festubert (April and May 1915); diversions for the Battle of Loos (September 1915) and at Fromelles (July 1916), all came to nothing. Between these sporadic periods of fighting, the day to day grind of static trench warfare continued. In places - notoriously at Givenchy but also at Neuve Chapelle and Mauquissart - underground mine warfare added a particular form of tension and horror, as did the German use of poison gas in the second major battle around Ypres in April and May 1915. This aside, the German command in Flanders was generally content to strengthen its defences and to sit and wait while the British, Indian and Dominion forces spilled blood in tragically large quantities.

In the area south of Ypres, for two and a half years the British occupied an uncomfortable position on the lower slopes of the Wytschaete-Messines ridge, overlooked at every point by German forces that were holding higher ground. On 7 June 1917, the ridge was quickly captured after an immense artillery bombardment and the explosion of nineteen long-prepared and very large mine charges. The position to which the British Second Army advanced during this action, the Battle of Messines, remained largely unchanged for the next ten months and became the front line when the German attacked in the Battle of the Lys in April 1918. The capture of the ridge was seen as a vital preparatory step before the British launched a major offensive designed to break out of the confines of the salient around Ypres and ultimately to clear the enemy from the Belgian coast. There were many salients during the war, but the British knew of only one Salient, that of Ypres.

Commencing on 31 July 1917 and lasting until the bitter, wet November, this Third Battle of Ypres proved to be a terribly costly failure, achieving little except to wear down German resources and push the line a few kilometres further from the city. One thing it did achieve, coupled with other factors, such as the US entry into the war in April 1917, was that the Germans realised that a war conducted purely on strong defence lines (as had largely been the case of the Western Front) was no longer viable, even with operational changes, such as the use of counter-attack divisions. The huge growth in artillery, amongst other factors, meant that no line, no matter how strong, could withstand a determined offensive. Nowhere is this more clearly shown in practical terms than in the effective abandonment of constructing new, robust defence lines at the conclusion of Third Ypres. If a decisive military result was to be obtained before a skilled (as opposed to a large) American army developed on the scene, probably by mid 1919, decisive action had to be taken as soon as practicable in 1918. The favourable ending of the war with Russia on the Eastern Front provided the essential resources for such action.

The relatively static nature of the war in the area between Ypres and Armentières up to April 1918 confined the concentrated destructive effect of fighting to a narrow strip of land – perhaps three kilometres deep on either side of the entrenched front. Only in the area between Wytschaete and Messines had there been any significant movement, which created a somewhat deeper devastated zone. Long range shell fire and aerial bombardment took a toll in the rear areas, yet on the allied side many of the local people, the population swelled by refugees from central Belgium, decided to stay rather than flee to the west. The whole panoply

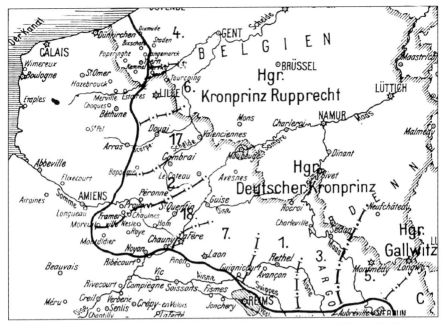

The general situation on the Western Front after Operation 'Michael'. The Lys offensive would be undertaken by the *Sixth* and *Fourth Armies*.

of war built up behind the fighting front, in and around the villages: bivouac and hutted camps; stores and dumps; headquarters and billets; water supply facilities; airfields; motor transport parks; medical units; artillery battery positions and ammunition stores.

German plans and intentions.

After the decisive defeat of their attack on France in 1914, continuous fighting on Germany's Western Front had achieved nothing of strategic significance. The years of trench warfare and the epic battles at Ypres, Artois, the Somme, the Chemin des Dames, in the Champagne, the Argonne and at Verdun had greatly worn down both sides in manpower and economically. The war had gone on much longer and on a much greater scale than any pre-war military planner, politician or financier could have predicted, yet such was the depth and ingenuity of the Great Powers that there was still much in reserve. It would be events elsewhere that provided fresh impetus.

On 7 November 1917 the Bolshevik Military Revolutionary Committee directed the commencement of armed revolution in Russia, overthrowing the Provisional Government. Next day, the new leadership passed the 'Decree of Peace', calling for the end of war with Germany and Austria-Hungary and for a just and democratic peace. Russia was in effect withdrawing from the war, although it would take some months of bitter wrangling before Germany imposed the crushing terms of the Treaty of Brest-Litovsk on the new Russian Government. Four days later – and ironically exactly a year before the Armistice of 11 November 1918 - Germany's *de facto* military commander, General Erich Ludendorff, met with Generals von Kuhl and von der Schulenberg (chiefs of staff to the Crown Princes Rupprecht and Wilhelm's Groups of Armies respectively) in a pre-planned meeting at Mons to consider their strategy. Ludendorff was already inclined to take the offensive:

> 'The Army had come victoriously through 1917; but it had become apparent that the holding of the Western Front purely by a defensive could no longer be counted on, in view of the enormous quantity of material of all kinds which the Entente had now at their disposal. Even where tactical conditions had been absolutely normal, and by no means so unfavourable as in the struggle for the Wytschaete salient or Laffaux Corner, we had lost ground and suffered heavily. These losses had indeed been greater than we had incurred in well-conducted attacks. The enormous material resources of the enemy had given his attack a considerable preponderance over our defence, and this condition would become more and more apparent as our best men became casualties, our infantry approximated more nearly in character to a militia, and discipline declined.'
>
> (Ludendorff, *My War Memories*)

Developments in Russia added a new dimension as revolution led to the end of fighting on what had been Germany's Eastern Front. The possibility, soon to become certainty, of being able to move large forces from there to the Western Front gave the Germans a potentially decisive advantage in terms of manpower and artillery. Opinions were divided on the best approach to exploit this advantage and the planners were sent away to devise options and alternatives. The Mons meeting was the genesis of what would become the Battle of the Lys, for von Kuhl proposed a strike against the British in Flanders.

The United States of America had entered the war on the allied side on 6 April 1917; but its military presence in Europe was taking time to build. Drawing upon vast resources, it was, however, only a matter of quite when the continued arrival of the 'Doughboys' in France would tip the scale back in the allies favour. The German General Staff at the *Oberste Heeres Leitung* (OHL: General Headquarters) recognised this

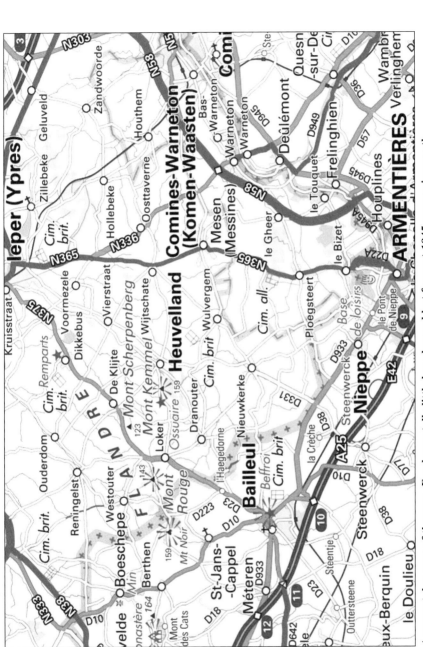

A present day map of the area. Fundamentally little has changed but for post-1945 economic growth.

and concluded that their offensive operations were urgent: there was an opportunity of a few months in the spring of 1918, no more.

The approach that emerged was that the German Armies in France and Flanders would seize the initiative and launch a series of offensives aimed squarely at the defeat of the British. The first, Operation Michael, was launched on 21 March 1918. It had an important effect on planning for future operations in Flanders in that it consumed much greater military resources than had initially been foreseen. In consequence, the Flanders operation was scaled down and orders to this effect were given on 23 March. Five days later, the Germans launched Operation Mars in the Arras area; a costly failure. Had Flanders been given precedence and resources, the whole pattern of events described in this book may have been very much different to the way things worked out – and it remains one of the intriguing 'what ifs' of the Great War. Ludendorff met with the staffs of the *Fourth* and *Sixth Armies* of Rupprecht's *Group* on 3 April, finalising the scale and objectives of the offensive now known as Operation Georgette. That the attack began just six days later is a reflection of the prodigious logistical effort of assembling the huge forces involved.

Objectives.

The 'Georgette' attack was to be carried out by the *Sixth Army* (von Quast) and part of the *Fourth* (Sixt von Arnim), employing a total of nineteen divisions on a frontage of some twenty-three miles (thirty-seven kilometres). *Sixth Army* was to reach Hazebrouck and to seize the complex of railways by which the British Second Army in Flanders was supplied. A little further east, *Fourth Army* would also reach the main supply road that ran from Steenvoorde to Poperinge and fed the same army in the Ypres area. Their advance would also seize the summits of the chain of low hills, the most important of which was Kemmel, from which the rear of the Second Army area could be dominated. In other words, success in these objectives would strangle supply into the Ypres sector and begin to force the Second Army into a pocket. If all went well, further advances could isolate that army and destroy it in detail. The Channel ports of Dunkirk, Calais and Boulogne – only a hundred kilometres at most from the present front - might also be reached, with devastating consequences for the rest of the British Expeditionary Force and for the allies in total. On the left of the *Sixth Army's* attack, a wheeling movement would bring German forces in behind Béthune and the British First Army. Possibilities might then develop for further offensive operations to destroy that Army, too.

That the German offensive failed to achieve its objectives is explained

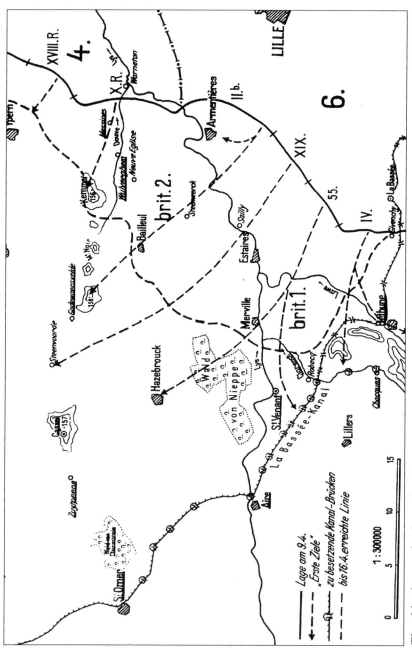

The objectives set for Operation 'Georgette' included the railways at Hazebrouck; the high ground of the Flemish Hills; and the La Bassée Canal to enable a sweep behind Béthune.

7

in detail in this book, but how geographically close it came may be judged by the forced British abandonment of the key railway depots north of Borre, which is just outside Hazebrouck, and the loss to the Germans of the geographic bastion of defence in Flanders, Kemmelberg Hill. It also led to a reluctant but absolutely necessary withdrawal from the Passchendaele line, won at such human cost and effort in 1917.

The Lys was a single battle but the nature of the terrain and that the attack frontage straddled two German Armies placed it in two quite contrasting regions with characteristically different fighting and outcomes. This volume focuses on the *Fourth Army*. It came into action on 10 April 1918, the day after *Sixth Army* had attacked on its left and, most encouragingly, had already crossed the Lys.

Tactics.
Although the German Armies in France had not been on the general offensive in France since 1917, they had been developing tactics for it. Even by the German attack at Verdun in early 1916, the army increasingly practiced the separation of specialist assault and trench-holding formations. Small unit command and control, mobile firepower, and battlefield tactics that promoted the concept of infiltration all developed rapidly. Perhaps the most important aspect of the 1918 offensive approach was that of the artillery. Developed through practice in Operation Strandfest at Nieuport and at Riga in 1917, it provided a way for the enemy's response to a German attack to be neutralised or rendered ineffective for long enough for the attack to succeed. By 'Georgette', the offensive capability of the Germans was at a peak.

But it had a serious weakness: there was no genuine means of exploitation. The Germans had developed no armoured capability to speak of; it had relatively few and largely untested cavalry; and it relied greatly on horse transport. Its advance would be only as far and as fast as man could go on foot. This flaw would prove to be its undoing on the Lys.

The British on the Defensive.
Just at the very moment that OHL was seizing the initiative and planning how to use the resources from Russia, the British were at a low point. Their major offensive efforts on the Somme (1916), at Arras (April 1917), Ypres (July to November) and Cambrai (November) were perceived by many to have achieved little other than the squandering of men's lives. It was certainly not an adequate return for enormous national effort. Disappointment gave added voice to those who believed that the war could not be won on the Western Front at all, and that the vast resources

The Germans assembled large forces for the 'Georgette' offensive but they were of uneven quality. (Author)

of Empire would be more effectively used in Salonika, Palestine and Mesopotamia.

With the British General Headquarters in France (GHQ) under Field Marshal Sir Douglas Haig already complaining of a lack of manpower, Prime Minister David Lloyd George rather perversely agreed with the French that the British should take over another twenty-six kilometres of the front line. First mooted at the Anglo-French Conference in Boulogne in September 1917, Haig was asked to consider it. He reported back on 8 October, insisting that in view of the currently doubtful power of the French army to resist a German attack, all other British fronts should be placed on the defensive; the sixty-two divisions of the BEF now in France should be brought up to full strength, and the occupied line should not be extended. Political will was not running in Haig's favour and French Commander-in-Chief Philippe Pétain asked the British to relieve his Sixth Army down as far as Barisis, which meant an extra front requiring six more divisions in the front line. Haig said he would do his best, but knew that this move was the end of aspirations for continuation of the offensive.

On 3 December, Haig ordered all of his Army Commanders to organise their zones for defensive purposes. Later that month, new French Prime Minister Georges Clemenceau began to press for the British to take on an extra and wholly impractical sixty kilometres of line. The German offensives intervened before any agreement had been reached.

A new approach to defence.

The British had not been on the defensive since 1914 but had much hard experience of facing effective German defence in action. GHQ issued new guidelines on 14 December 1917, entitled 'Memorandum on defensive measures'. It outlined the British adoption of defensive principles that had been applied so successfully by the Germans in 1917. The front would no longer be protected by a number of continuous trench lines but would consist of deep defensive zones, 'with the main resistance being made on ground favourable to us'. The enemy would have to negotiate intensive cross fire from well sited, sheltered and barbed-wire protected strong points, held by tenacious troops. Should the enemy penetrate the first zones and beat off local counter attacks, strong reserves would strike at them with a major counter attack and ideally go on not only to recover the ground but inflict defeat. The concept of such 'elastic' defence in depth was unfamiliar to the British way of thinking: up to now the general instruction if attacked had been hold to the line; close any gaps; give not an inch of ground. The new approach demanded a great deal of consideration of the battlefield terrain and re-training of officers and men alike. It also required the physical construction of an entirely new system of defences – but as it was not yet understood where the Germans would attack, this meant that the entire British front had to be reconsidered and rebuilt, at the same time that the existing trenches needed to be manned and on the alert. Considered in retrospect, the British were in a race against time, but intelligence did not indicate an early attack in French Flanders and little work was done in this area on modifying the defensive position for the new doctrine.

The British interpretation of the German method tended to place far more men into the Forward Zone and consequently fewer in reserve ready for fighting in the Battle Zone or for moving up from the Rear Zone. There was lack of clarity with regard to who could authorise withdrawal from the forward positions, and when this should be done. For instance, on 1 April 1918 Lieutenant General John du Cane, commanding XV Corps in the Lys area, made it clear that there would be 'no retirement of any sort without an order from higher authority. Posts would be defended to the last regardless of consequences.'

The combination of these factors would have baleful consequences for the front line troops of the British Army during the German offensive.

Reorganisation of the BEF in progress.

During the first three months of 1918 the British Army in France and Flanders underwent considerable organisational change, and was still in the process of coming to terms with new ways when the German attacks began. Shortage of infantry manpower was addressed by the drastic measure of cutting the number of battalions in each brigade from four to three. Many battalions were disbanded, in a disruptive move guaranteed to affect *esprit de corps*. It also meant that in future the battalions had to be rotated between front line, support and reserve positions more frequently than before. In addition to this, the brigades lost their Machine Gun Company as they were merged into a single Machine Gun Battalion within each division. GHQ itself underwent considerable turmoil, as political pressure led to the replacement of some of Haig's senior staff advisers and the Lloyd George-inspired installation of a wholly separate advisory body in the form of the Supreme War Council. At the War Office, the Chief of the Imperial General Staff, General Sir William Robertson, for much of the war a staunch supporter of GHQ and Haig, was forced out and replaced in February 1918 by the wily soldier-politician, General Sir Henry Wilson.

A 'cushy' sector.

When the German attack in Flanders began on 9 April 1918 and was extended next day, it faced seven allied divisions: six British and one Portuguese. Of the British, five of those divisions had just arrived in the area, having been very recently heavily engaged in the fighting against Operation Michael further south. When opportunity had come to relieve these shattered formations, they were sent to Flanders to rebuild. The Armentières to Ploegsteert sector had the reputation since 1914 of being a cushy sector, to the extent that it was used to give new units straight out from the training camps in Britain their first taste of life in the trenches. This was certainly not the case as one approached closer to Ypres, but there had been no major fighting in this sector since the summer of 1917 and nothing was expected. The last of the forces that would be engaged in 'Georgette' to arrive was the 9th (Scottish) Division, which only reached the area on 1 April, whilst its artillery was still pulling in two days later.

During the battle, another one Australian and eight British divisions arrived. Three of them had also been through the mill in Operation Michael. Only one, the 1st Australian Division, could reasonably be

Armentières was a key bridging point across the Lys and had been regarded as a relatively quiet sector until April 1918. (Author)

described as fresh, for its last major action had been back in September 1917. It took its place in the area between the Forest of Nieppe and Strazeele; out of the area covered by this book.

Most of the infantry units of the newly arrived divisions had received (or were receiving) large new drafts of men to take the place of recent casualties. In the main they were 'A4 men': soldiers aged eighteen and a half who had been in training but were now suddenly rushed to France as reinforcements. Many units were still assimilating these green arrivals and sorting out their interior organisation when 'Georgette' struck.

On 3 April 1918, while inspecting units of the 9th (Scottish) Division, General Sir Herbert Plumer, commanding Second Army, told the men that they need not be concerned about a German attack in Flanders, for they had neither the men nor the guns for such an enterprise. Poor military intelligence, an over-optimistic reading of the situation, or propaganda? We shall see. Even so, there was a general feeling that the Germans would attack at some point, and steps were taken to ensure that no large dumps of ammunition were kept in the forward area, lest they be captured. It was a decision that would affect the front line units when the attack did come and cost many drivers of horsed and mechanical transport their lives when they attempted to maintain supply when under fire.

Battlefield Topography
The *Fourth Army's* plan of attack took it in a broadly north westerly

12

direction. At the southern end of its front, with *Sixth Army* on its left, lay Armentières. A large, light industrial town, it had the misfortune of being very close to the front line trenches since late in 1914 and in consequence had suffered its share of destruction by shellfire. Despite the evident dangers, the buildings and cellars of the town had been constantly used by the British for billeting, medical facilities, stores, headquarters and signals stations. Large numbers of local people, their numbers swelled by refugees from Lille and further afield, remained present – at least until 21 July 1917 when, during the German Operation *Totendanz* (Dance of Death), the town was heavily shelled with mustard gas. Some 6,400 civilians and soldiers were affected by it. The exercise was repeated a week later. But there was worse to come. On 7 April 1918, the town, along with nearby La Chapelle d'Armentières and Nouvel Houplines, was subjected to a gas bombardment ten and a half hours long, fired by the artillery of the Saxon *32nd Infanterie-Division*, soaking it with the contents of between 25 and 40,000 mustard gas shells to such an extent that it rendered the town uninhabitable for at least a fortnight. The British 34th Division, which was holding the Armentières front at the time, sustained some 900 gas casualties. The reason for this bombardment was the forthcoming Operation Georgette. Mustard gas was a ground-denial weapon; it rendered the gassed area dangerous or lethal for troops. Retreat from the town would be no easy matter, for the looping Lys passed across its northern outskirts, with relatively few bridges. The gas shelling of Armentières was to deny it to the British: and the reason for that was that neither *Sixth* nor *Fourth Army* was going to attack it directly, with the two quickly by-passing it on the north and south flanks respectively. Speed of advance was the essence, and OHL had no desire to become embroiled in difficult street fighting. Armentières would simply be pinched out and would fall as the two Armies moved beyond it: infiltration on the grand scale.

North west of Armentières the ground rises to the dominating Flemish Hills. Rarely reaching a height of more than 150 metres, the chain of peaks looks down eastwards upon the flat and often wet Lys valley and provides the occupying observer with a perfect view of the entire battlefield. On a fine day it is often possible to see as far southwards as Vimy Ridge and the Lorette Spur, not far north of Arras, and across as far as Lille. On the northern side of these hills, the ground drops away towards Godewaersvelde, Poperinge and ultimately to Ypres itself. The North Sea coast can often be seen from the heights. From the Mont des Cats (situated behind Méteren and, as such, situated just outside the geographic scope of this book) eastwards through Mont Noir, Mont

Rouge, the Scherpenberg and Kemmelberg, the military importance of these hills is hard to over-state.

East of the hills the ground gently undulates across rich farmland. For the German attack it meant an initial uphill advance to Messines Ridge, which is crowned by the road running south from Ypres through St Eloi, Wytschaete, Messines, Ploegsteert and Le Bizet into Armentières. Once on the ridge, the attack would take it down a gradual slope before another climb to high ground surmounted by Neuve Église. This provides the occupier with a fine view back across the valley to Messines Ridge. The whole area was riddled by the trenches, barbed wire, dugouts, shell holes and mine craters of earlier fighting.

South of Messines the ridge road gently drops away southwards to the valley of the little River Douve. This is an eastward flowing tributary that joins the Lys at Warneton and is the only waterway of any great significance in the battle area: it is only perhaps one or two metres across during the summer, but is often swollen by winter rain and melt. As it is orientated in a west-east direction, the Douve did not present any great military barrier to German intentions.

Southwards from the Douve valley, the ground once again rises, this time to a prominence known to the British as Hill 63. From this height there is an excellent view eastwards across the mass of Ploegsteert Wood. The only dense woodland of any great size within the battle area, it had been used since 1914 for the shelter of troops that were in reserve to the front line trenches that skirted its eastern face. The wood was cut through by tracks and rides but would present an obstacle for any major military force that needed to pass through it: but, as with Armentières, the *Fourth Army* thought better of it and simply planned to outflank the wood on either side.

Operational matters

Fourth Army's initial attack on 10 April 1918 was a much smaller affair than that carried out by *Sixth Army* the day before. It deployed only four front line divisions on a seventeen kilometres front, compared *to Sixth Army's* fifteen divisions over twenty-seven kilometres, with another four in deep reserve. Over the attack frontage, while *Sixth Army's* density was about the same as used in 'Michael' (fifty-three divisions over 103 kilometres), *Fourth Army* was prepared only for a much smaller operation, so much so that it could almost be considered only as a wing of *Sixth Army's* battle.

The assault forces were disposed as follows, south to north:

Fourth Army [Sixt von Arnim]
X Reserve Corps [von Eberhardt]
Faced the British 25th Division between Frélinghien and the Douve River.
Deployed four divisions. In front, *31st and 214th Divisions. 22nd Reserve Division and 11th Bavarian Division* in reserve.

XVIII Corps [Sieger]
Faced the 19th (Western) and 9th (Scottish) Divisions from the Douve River northwards.
Deployed *17th Reserve and 7th Divisions*, both in front, with *36th and 49th Reserve Divisions* in reserve.

Fourth Army's own artillery had been supplemented by the arrival of more resources released from 'Michael' and by some guns transferred overnight from *Sixth Army*, but the density of guns also reflected planning for a much smaller operation. In total, it could array 522 guns, of which 215 were classified as heavy or super heavy. In terms of guns per kilometre of front to be assaulted, this was well below (less than two-thirds) the force employed at the start of the previous major attacks ('Michael' 6608 guns for 103 kilometres; *Sixth Army* on 9 April, 1686 for twenty-seven kilometres) but, even so, it considerably out-gunned the British.

Having guns in place is one thing; supplying and moving them forwards quite another. The rush to move forces and materiel into the 'Georgette' area placed much strain onto the German railway and transport system. As late as 7 April, Rupprecht was complaining that his Group of Armies was receiving only half of the eight to ten ammunition trains that it needed per day. On average, the divisions being moved into place for the attack were also short of 600 horses each.

To face this onslaught, the British Second Army (Plumer) included just three divisions in the front line, with no others in close reserve. All had recently arrived after suffering serious losses during 'Michael'.

IX Corps [Hamilton-Gordon]
25th Division [Bainbridge], 19th (Western) Division [Jeffreys].
XXII Corps (formerly II ANZAC) [Godley]
9th (Scottish) Division [Tudor].

Early in the great crisis of Operation Michael, Ferdinand Foch had been appointed as a co-ordinating Generalissimo, effectively in operational command of the French and British armies, although it was not until a further agreement, made at Beauvais on 3 April, that he was placed in overall strategic command. It was a new and politically sensitive arrangement. Haig began badgering him for French reserves and, despite this falling on deaf ears, stepped up his demands once 'Georgette' began. It was, for some time, a stand-off. Haig, whose personal relationships with Foch were generally amicable, ran into the Frenchman's three-part dictum for the conduct of a battle: 'Never withdraw, Never relieve tired troops while the battle lasts [and] One does what one can.' Foch never tired of stressing these maxims and his assistant Weygand faithfully represented them. They became an unchallengeable dictum and lay behind all of Foch's advice and orders to the British. It took a while for the fundamental logic to sink in to the men in khaki, and at times of greatest stress during the remainder of the German offensives they often perplexed and frustrated the British staff. These three simple phrases dictated the course of the Allied defence on the Somme and on the Lys.

In practice, Foch's response to Haig forced the latter to take every possible step to fight the battle with his own resources. Eventually, Foch recognised that a dangerous tipping point was being reached and he deployed French forces to what proved to be the final phases of battle.

Chapter Two

The Battles of the Lys
1918

Overview.
After the war, when it defined geographic limits, dates and which
formations and units had taken part, the British Battles Nomenclature
Committee broke the Lys fighting down into eight phases. For ease of
understanding, these are not used in this book but are given in an
Appendix. Instead, it shall be considered in three phases.

Phase 1:
On 9 April 1918 *Sixth Army's* attack broke the allied front in the area
held by the 2nd Portuguese and the 40th Divisions; and by day's end had
forced a significant crossing of the Lys at Bac St Maur and a more
tenuous one across the Lawe at the Rault Lock. Next day, progress was
made in both areas. On the northern bank of the Lys, the towns of
Merville and Estaires fell into enemy hands. The attack was broadened
on 10 April to include *Fourth Army* and progress was made in the
Ploegsteert and Messines area against the 19th (Western) and the 25th
Divisions. With the Germans advancing on both sides of it, Armentières,
which had been subjected to heavy gas bombardment but not frontally
attacked, was now threatened with encirclement and a decision was
taken to evacuate the town. All of the divisions of the British XI, XV
and IX Corps were now fully committed to the battle and many of the
units that had been in the Forward and Battle Zones were already
reduced to remnants. In the areas behind the fighting front, mass
withdrawal of the facilities and units of the lines of communication
began: the roads were also full of civilian refugees fleeing the area. On
the extremities of the front that was attacked, the British held their
ground: in the south at Givenchy, the Territorials of the well-drilled 55th
(West Lancashire) Division recaptured the village after initial German
penetration; in the north and only just outside Ypres, the 9th (Scottish)
Division gave little ground.

Many men of the British units that were holding the Forward Zone when the offensive began were captured through the sheer rapidity of the German advance. (Author)

Phase 2:

As early as 9 April, other divisions – mainly from the Ypres area – were rushed to the Lys sector to stem the German attack. The 49th (West Riding) and the 59th (2nd North Midland) divisions arrived to reinforce in Second Army's area. In such an urgent and increasingly critical situation, they were deployed piecemeal, with battalions being sent into action as individual units. They met with the difficult problem of not knowing exactly where the enemy was, understanding only that parts of British units were fighting somewhere ahead of them. Most of them encountered broken units and men streaming back from the battle before they came under fire. There was now no line as such. The battle became fragmented, with actions taking place at the same time on different parts of the field as units and parts of units were desperately deployed. Almost inevitably, as German pressure continued and British units found themselves outnumbered and out-gunned, many of the newly arrived units suffered the same fate as those originally attacked. There were numerous examples of localised heroic last stand actions that bought precious time. The Germans made much slower progress as they pressed on north of Armentières into the more defensible Flemish Hills. After hard fights for

Neuve Église and Ravelsberg Hill, the town of Bailleul – since 1914 a key British headquarters, medical and airfield centre – was occupied by the Germans and then largely destroyed by British artillery and bombing. Pleas from the British high command for French reinforcements fell, at least at first, largely on deaf ears, for it was generally believed that the Germans were also about to attack elsewhere. Field Marshal Sir Douglas Haig issued his well known 'backs to the wall' order during this phase, and serious plans were considered for flooding the area in front of Dunkirk as a final back-stop should the Germans continue to make progress.

Phase 3:
While the first reinforcement divisions were being fed into the battle, others were being ordered to the area. With the British Armies now being at full stretch, it was found necessary to shorten the front line around Ypres in order to reduce the number of men required to hold it. This was a bitter moment indeed, for the ground won at such hideous cost in 1917 – and more - was evacuated without a fight in order for this to take place. In addition to this, the 1st Australian Division was moved by train from the Somme: it advanced through the Forest of Nieppe, determined to hold a line. On the Australians' left, several French divisions arrived and formed a line north of Bailleul. On the Australians' right, the British 5th, 1st and 4th divisions arrived and held the line of the Forest and down along the La Bassée Canal. By mid-April, the *Sixth Army* had been brought to a halt, well short of its battle objectives. It was, not yet known to the British, reaching the end of its capabilities. A tactical pause slowed the fighting for some time and no further progress of any significance was made in that Army's area. Late in April, fresh German divisions in *Fourth Army's* area assaulted and captured Kemmelberg Hill in one of the finest feats of arms of the war, bringing fresh concern to the allies. A further effort to press on to the next hill, the Scherpenberg, was halted mainly by French forces and attacks closer to Ypres were blunted by stubborn British resistance. A decision was taken to abandon Operation Georgette.

Chapter Three

Breakthrough at Ploegsteert
10–11 April 1918

The German attack in Flanders came as something of a surprise, not least because of the received opinion that Flanders was generally too wet for a large-scale action this early in the year. There had been signs of a German build-up: trains and columns of men had been seen from the air, and much noise of movement heard at night, but no intelligence from trench raids or prisoners gave a clear indication of intent. Even once the attack began with such violence, the British high command was still not convinced that it was anything but a large scale diversion to an attack that was expected at Arras. It initially hesitated to commit too many of its reserves, and it was only when the German attack extended north on the second day that reality began to dawn.

News of the German attack south of Armentières on 9 April came as no surprise to the British troops of the 25th Division north of the town, for to their right they clearly heard the fury of the hours of bombardment. A close watch was kept on their front, but there was no unusual sign of any German activity. Behind the lines, Alexander Hamilton-Gordon, commanding IX Corps and widely known amongst his officers as 'Sunny Jim', due to a somewhat morose nature, sent the 25th Division's reserve 74 Brigade to assist in stemming the attack; but in general there was no cause for concern on his own Corps' front. His staff officer GSO2, the then Major Bernard Law Montgomery DSO, went off to Cassel to attend a planned Second Army conference on training.

At 2.45am, in the gathering mist and rain of the next morning, the massed guns of the *Fourth Army* opened up as one, commencing a four and a half hour bombardment programme. For the first two hours, it aimed in depth at the British artillery, headquarters and communication, a large proportion of the shells fired were *Buntkreuz*, containing a mixture of chemicals, including phosgene. Men fought much of this day wearing respirators. Soon enough, many of the British batteries were reporting that all telephone wires were cut; and in the dark, smoke and fog, visual signalling was almost out of the question. In some areas a complex, deep-buried, cable network and wireless systems kept the British command

Ploegsteert – 'Plug Street' to the Tommies – was close behind the front line but had been safe enough for billeting troops since 1914. The *Aux trois amis* estaminet was a favourite. (Author)

system in communication. Some fifty minutes after the bombardment began, some German guns turned onto the British front line trenches and posts, employing high explosive and 'Blue Cross': a chemical weapon consisting mainly of Diphenylchloroarsine, a particulate designed to irritate to such an extent that it would force men to remove their respirators. The next two and a half hours were aimed at the continued destruction and neutralisation of the British ability to respond to attack, with especial concentration on reserve trenches and places where infantry might assemble ready to counter-attack. Finally, after five minutes of concentrated fire on the British front line, the field guns switched to producing a creeping barrage, behind which the German assault infantry would advance.

Hamilton-Gordon's Corps held the line with two divisions: from its right on the River Lys near Frélinghien, north as far as the River Douve, the 25th Division was in position, holding its front with two brigades. It was unaware that *XVIII Corps* had moved its *31st and 214th Divisions* into place ready to attack the two brigades, and had *49th Reserve Division* close enough to support the attack. Across the Douve and continuing the line up to the Wambeke stream came the 19th (Western) Division. Both the British divisions had recently arrived after being badly mauled during Operation Michael. The battle fought by the 19th (Western) Division will

21

be examined in the section on the fight for Messines Ridge, while the rest of this section describes the 25th Division and its battle for Ploegsteert.

The front line held by the 25th Division lay on the western bank of the Lys, in marshy ground that was pitted with the shell holes, trenches and dugouts of previous years. With no continuous front line worthy of the name, the division manned its front by defensive posts, often widely separated. The German front line lay on the far side of the river, with only the road bridge at Frélinghien and railway bridge at Nouvel Houplines as permanent structures by which heavy traffic could cross.

Late on 9 April, as it was becoming known that the Germans had crossed the Lys at Bac St Maur on the far side of Armentières, Divisional HQ took steps to form a 'brigade group' to make a defensive flank facing Armentières. It ordered its 6/South Wales Borderers (pioneer battalion), with half of 2/South Lancashire, a detachment of the divisional Machine Gun Battalion and the division's three Royal Engineers' Field Companies to move and concentrate on a line between Le Bizet and Vanne. Preparations were made to blow up the railway bridge, at the discretion of 75 Brigade, while all others would be destroyed only on IX Corps' orders.

75 Brigade

The right-hand sector of the division's front was held by the 8/Border and 11/Cheshires of 75 Brigade, with the brigade's third battalion, 2/South Lancashire, in reserve. The brigade held an unusually long front of some 3,200m, stretching from Lys Farm up to the east of Le Gheer. The land is flat, open and dotted with farms, most of which had been used by the British army for billets and headquarters since 1914, except for the area behind the Cheshires, which included the southern side of Ploegsteert Wood.

Well into the rear, Ploegsteert village and the Franco-Belgian border village of Le Bizet were the only significant built-up areas behind 75 Brigade; behind them came the huts and tents of army camps massed around Romarin. Beyond that, the way lay open to the high ground of Neuve Église and Bailleul. On the brigade's right was the 34th Division, holding Armentières, the northern outskirts of which reached almost to Le Bizet.

The 8/Border reported that things were quiet, other than for some shellfire and an annoying German machine gun, firing constantly from Frélinghien in the direction of battalion headquarters at Despierre Farm. They thought that this was not so much to harass them as to cover the sound of working parties. This is possibly true, for at night the Germans were quietly building plank bridges just below the surface of the Lys. On the night before the attack broke, three patrols went out: one from A

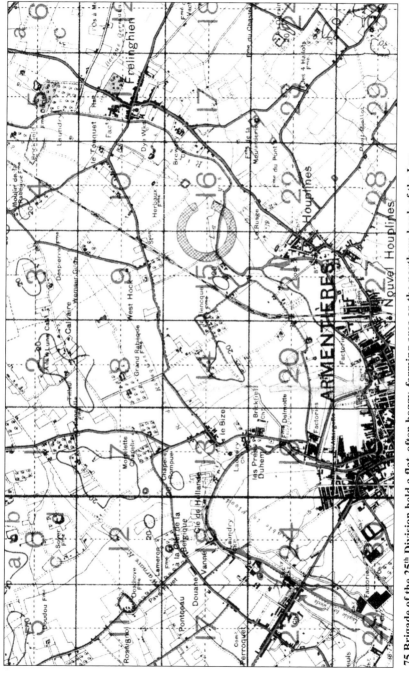

75 Brigade of the 25th Division held a flat, often boggy, farming area on the northern bank of the Lys.

Company was never heard of again, but the others came back with nothing of importance to report. Even as late as 6am on 10 April, A Company – which was on the left, next to the Cheshires - was signalling to Lieutenant Colonel Charles Birt at headquarters that all was well.

Australian Lieutenant Colonel Charles Birt commanded 8/Border Regiment throughout the battle. (Author)

10 April
Things changed very quickly. German infantry loomed out of the thick mist, rapidly enveloping the forward posts. Initial reports from the front line units do not make for a wholly coherent story, but it appears that the point of first penetration was on the extreme right of the area held by the 8/Border, for by 5.30am German troops were advancing up Railway Switch from the Lys Farm area. At about the same time, the Cheshires heard that the enemy had reached Le Touquet Station. Their presence there immediately imperilled the two British battalions, threatening to cut off and destroy the companies in the front line area by advancing northwards across their rear.

After the battle and when there was opportunity to review what had taken place, it was said that German officers, to keep their men in touch, led with a white handkerchief or cloth tied to a stick; everyone said that their machine gunners were thrust well forward; that the Germans fired Very lights on reaching a position; others then rushed up to it. In most cases, British troops in rapid withdrawal had to rely on verbal communications, which were 'invariably confused and misleading', and nowhere more so than on the flanks, where communication between units was often non-existent.

By 5.50am the 11/Cheshires were also being attacked, but from their left: the result of enemy progress against 7 Brigade. Germans were also seen in the rear of battalion headquarters, causing it to withdraw to the cover of the wood, all the while under fire from Lancashire Support Farm. The front to the east of that farm had been held by the Borders' A Company, of which little more was heard except that Second Lieutenant William Preston, Company Sergeant Major 5069 James Gent and about twenty men had been driven back to the wood, where they came into contact with elements of the 1/Wiltshire of 7 Brigade. Soon afterwards, Preston was killed (Pte John Sheehan later wrote to his mother, saying that William was the victim of a sniper); Gent continued to play a central part in his company's work during the battle and was awarded the Distinguished Conduct Medal for his exploits. The citation reads,

'When all the officers of his company had become casualties this warrant officer took command and reorganised it. He remained in command for four days, fighting a rearguard action the whole time. His magnificent example of courage and coolness against overwhelming odds inspired his men to a stubborn resistance, reducing his own casualties, and inflicting heavy losses on, and checking, the enemy.'

Second Lieutenant John Allan, who had been in command of A Company, was also killed: along with another eighty of the eighty-three officers and men of his battalion who lost their lives on this day, he has no known grave.

The Borders' two reserve companies, C and D, had been assembled on a line from Lys Farm to Gunners Farm. Soon after the attack began, Birt sent all spare men from headquarters down Nicholson's Avenue to get into touch with them. They may have been fortunate, for by 6.45am Despierre Farm was cut off from front and rear: there was nothing for it but for Birt and his headquarters to either try to join 11/Cheshire somewhere in Ploegsteert Wood or make for Le Bizet and try to join up with the reserve companies. But the signs were that the Cheshires were in much the same plight, and Birt had no choice but to make a lengthy detour around the north of Ploegsteert. By the time he reached his two companies (and what was left of B Company, which had withdrawn from the forward posts to join them), the reserve line had been strengthened by the arrival of the 'brigade group', which had been ordered forwards from Vanne. Although the situation was serious, it was not devoid of hope as, at this time, the 34th Division over on the right was still holding Armentières and had not come under attack.

The attempt to counter-attack.
At 7am, the 'brigade group' in the area of Vanne received orders to concentrate at Chapelle Rompue, from where they were to counter-attack towards Lys Farm and Reserve Avenue. This advance was made under heavy shellfire, which caused serious casualties – made all the more galling by the fact that 75 Brigade had largely restored its situation except for its left, and the enemy attack was now developing at Ploegsteert. At 10am, brigade ordered the South Wales Borderers to withdraw back to Le Bizet: a move which undid any hopes of holding this ground, for it reduced the garrison holding the reserve line and with it all capability of mounting any serious counter-attack.

Birt went to report to brigade at Le Bizet and found that the Germans were now as far round on his left flank as Gasometer Corner. There was

25

The 25th Division responded to the attack, assembling reserves near Chapelle Rompue at Le Bizet. (Author)

nothing for it: they would have to fight their way out, and there were clashes in Le Bizet as the remnants of 8/Border attempted to get away. A German machine gun was captured but, without ammunition, it was just so much dead weight and was cast into a ditch. By 8am brigade was receiving news that the Germans were in the wood and advancing on Ploegsteert village. The headquarters and C and D Companies of the 2/South Lancashire were ordered to move forwards to take up a position across the Ploegsteert-Romarin road, about 2000 metres from Ploegsteert. Around 11am they were joined there by some hundred stragglers from 8/Border and shortly afterwards by the 6/South Wales Borderers and other elements of the 'brigade group'. On their right, a battalion loaned from the 19th (Western) Division, the 9/Cheshires, also came into line by 2pm and held the ground as far as Clef de Hollande, on the Lys bank west of Le Bizet. Things were reported as relatively quiet along this whole line; but they could see many Germans ahead of them, in and west of Ploegsteert, and many British stragglers came in from the battlefield ahead.

PLOEGSTEERT. — Rue de Messines.

Ploegsteert quickly fell into German hands on 10 April 1918. (Author)

During the afternoon, by which time the 34th Division was evacuating Armentières and withdrawing on the right of the 25th Division, a decision was taken to mount a counter-attack with the intention of recapturing Ploegsteert. The operation would be under the command of Lieutenant Colonel J. B. Allsopp of the South Lancashires. His orders were to clear the village and reach a line Touquet Berthe – 'Maison 1875' – Gunners Farm. Supported by a machine gun and short trench mortar barrage, the

27

attack by 2/South Lancashire and 6/South Wales Borderers commenced at 5.30pm: it proved to be a short and costly venture. Swept by German fire from ahead and also in enfilade from the direction of Le Bizet, the lead elements got to within 200 yards of the village but ultimately fell back towards Regina and Doudou Farms when an artillery barrage also began to fall, screening Ploegsteert from any further advance.

On the left of the two attacking battalions, the 1st Australian Army Troops Company of the Royal Engineers also attempted to advance their outposts, to ensure that there was no break in the line. They did so but were ordered to withdraw again when the counter-attack broke down. During this period nine men were wounded, but the company suffered a particularly great loss in the death of

Gallipoli veteran 'Ted' Falloon MM, killed during the attempt to recapture Ploegsteert. (Kerry Stokes Collection)

Company Sergeant Major Edward 'Ted' Falloon. A volunteer of August 1914 and a Gallipoli veteran who came from Richmond in Melbourne, he had twice earned the Military Medal in 1916. Without a known grave, Falloon is commemorated on the Villers-Bretonneux Memorial.

11 April

By the early hours of a very dark night, the right hand of the brigade's sector (from Oosthove Farm to Courte Rue, halfway to Nieppe) was being held by 9/Cheshires and what was left of the 8/Border, beyond which came 147 Brigade. They had been ordered to withdraw to this position after the attempted counter-attack on Ploegsteert had failed. There were no trenches or prepared defences in this area: the German push had turned the fighting into open warfare, and the battle of the next few days would be across farmland, dotted with the British camps and dumps that had until very recently been far away enough from the front to be safe from all but long-range or aerial bombardment.

Two heavy German attacks took place during the morning of 11 April, at 5.45am and 10.15am. Both were largely beaten off, with the important exception that in the second attack the German broke through the 9/Cheshires and 8/Border, and pushed on to the area south of Romarin. A machine gun, which proved troublesome, was brought forward to

Romarin had been far enough behind the trenches to be a significant site for British camps and stores, but it fell into German hands within hours. (Author)

Brune Gaye. The 6/South Wales Borders and 2/South Lancashire, both on the left of the Cheshires, fell back through Romarin, which was soon to fall into German hands. Mid-day attempts by these two battalions to recover the village were repelled.

During the evening, with the 34th Division now withdrawing from Nieppe, 75 Brigade was ordered to comply, taking it to a line running from the south of Romarin to Pont d'Achelles. It was to begin falling back at 8.30am, with battalions withdrawing one after the other, starting from the right. None was to move until the unit on its right hand had successfully retired. The move was completed successfully, although the precise situation at Romarin remained obscure and uncertain. Plans were raised next morning for a battalion of the newly arrived 100 Brigade (33rd Division), which had come up on the left of 75 Brigade, to attack Romarin – but this was soon cancelled when news came through that the enemy had broken through at Steenwerck, not far away across the Bailleul road and railway.

7 Brigade.

The much shorter left-hand sector of the 25th Division's front was held by 7 Brigade, which placed the 1/Wiltshire and 4/South Staffords in the front. The brigade's reserve battalion, 10/Cheshires, was positioned on the far side of Ploegsteert Wood, in the shelter of the network of dugouts

29

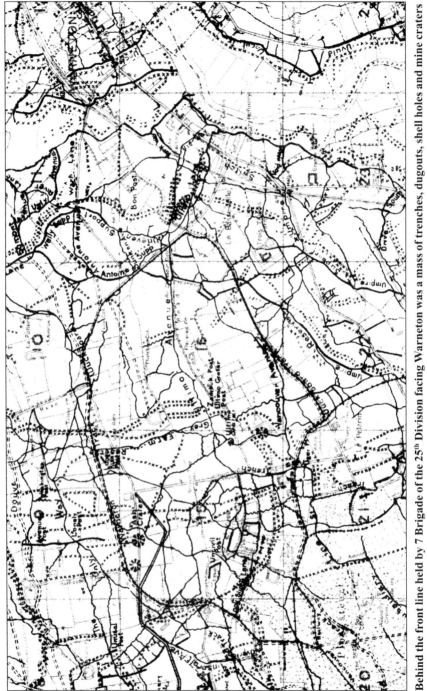

Behind the front line held by 7 Brigade of the 25th Division facing Warneton was a mass of trenches, dugouts, shell holes and mine craters from earlier fighting.

and tunnels below Hill 63 that was known as the Catacombs. The area between there and the front line was riddled with the trenches and barbed wire of previous periods, with light railways for supply and even a standard gauge railway spur for a 12-inch gun.

The Wiltshires' commanding officer was Lieutenant Colonel Sholto Stuart Ogilvie, who had enlisted in the ranks of the regiment in early September 1914. A barrister by profession, he had no previous military experience but had turned out to be a very fine soldier. Ogilvie, who was commissioned in the field in 1915, had twice been awarded the Distinguished Service Order and survived being wounded at Thiepval in 1916. He was still suffering the effects of the rheumatism that had affected him earlier in 1918. He placed only his A Company in the front line posts at La Basse-Ville (but strengthened it with an extra platoon on 9 April), with C and D forming his main line of defence further back, in Ultimo Avenue. B Company was held in reserve in the shelter of Ploegsteert Wood. Ogilvie set up his headquarters in the old Post Office at St Yves: alert to the possibility of attack, he ordered the battalion to stand to during the terrific German artillery bombardment in the early hours of 10 April.

Facing the Wiltshires, *Infanterie-Regiment 70* of *31st Infanterie-Division* prepared to make the assault. They had endured a miserable night's march in rain and fog, on wet, rutted and jammed roads, from Comines to Warneton and on the way suffered by shellfire the death of an officer, *Leutnant der Reserve* Helmuth Lilienfeld of 2/Machine Gun Company. He is now buried at the German cemetery at Wervik-Sud: his grave stands out, for it is below a Jewish headstone. The regiment placed its III Battalion on the left, facing the sugar factory at La Basse-Ville, and I Battalion on the right, nearer to Warneton.

At 5.10am the bombardment lifted from the Wiltshires' front line and within minutes it became necessary for A Company to fire an SOS signal rocket to call for assistance as German infantry loomed out of the mist. But no one saw the rocket in the gloom, no artillery response came, and runners were sent rearwards to take the urgent message. By good luck, a runner reached Ogilvie and he was able to put a telephone call through to the artillery. He also ordered B Company to reinforce C and D. By this time, A Company's four forward posts had already succumbed to III/IR70, and German troops were advancing northwards from the area held by 75 Brigade, cutting off the rest of the company. Despite Captain Frank Smith and his men of A Company doing their best to fight their way out, their supply of bullets and grenades soon ran short and at about 8.30am the remaining garrison of Smith and some thirty men surrendered.

On the left of the Wiltshires, the 4/South Staffs had a similar experience. This was an unusual unit that had spent up until October 1917 as a training battalion, but had gained much experience since and had, along with the rest of the division, come through the forge of Operation Michael. Its front line posts fired the SOS signal at 6am.

Second Lieutenant Sidney Morey, who had been one of the first to enlist into the pals of the first Birmingham City Battalion in 1914 before being commissioned three years later, was with C Company in the front line. He recalled that the battalion had been ordered to stand to during the bombardment, but it was impossible to see for more than twenty yards in the mist. A patrol sent out was 'evidently captured, as the first intimation we had of the attack was when we saw the enemy amongst our wire, throwing hand grenades into us'. Morey was one of many casualties in these first minutes of the German attack, being hit on the head by grenade splinters and suffering a severe wound to his leg, which included a fracture of the bone. Even so, 'when I managed to get up the enemy was mostly past us but I got another six rounds at them with my revolver … I rested for a few hours, bound myself up, and then tried to crawl through their lines.' This brave man was inevitably captured, spending seven months in hospital in Germany for treatment of his wounds and for sepsis. The battalion's records are too vague to tell us exactly where Morey was when he was hit, but the battalion's front line was near the river facing Warneton, and was attacked by *10. Lothringische Infanterie-Regiment 174* of *31st Infanterie-Division*, along with a company of *Sturmtrupp Koesters*, attached from *3. Hanseatisches Infanterie-Regiment Lübeck 162* from *17th Reserve-Division*, which was on the north side of the Douve.

Also with C Company in the front line was Second Lieutenant Alexander Walker, who had a similar background to Morey in that he had enlisted into the 7/Loyal North Lancashire and served for two years in the ranks in France: these officers were experienced and knew the ways of trench warfare. Even so, it was insufficient to help when, after his post had checked the first wave of German infantry through rifle fire, the second approached to within twenty yards, throwing grenades. Walker was wounded in the face and both legs, one being fractured. Immobile, within ten minutes he was in enemy hands.

The battalion's front very soon fell, and the German infantry advanced towards the main line at Watchful Post, La Potterie and Tilleul Farms. During the day, repeated attacks forced the abandonment of these locations; but the line was held along Grey Farm Trench, not far behind them and was linked up with the Wiltshires.

In reserve at the Catacombs, the 10/Cheshires survived the initial bombardment and at about 7am was ordered to form an outpost line 400 yards south across the Ypres-Armentières road and facing towards Ploegsteert. The line does not appear to have been seriously threatened (the Germans quite rightly looking to press on westwards rather than deal with it) but the battalion's C Company, especially, suffered casualties in exchanges of fire.

With the South Staffords holding on, the Wiltshires found it was their right flank that was under the most serious threat. Ogilvie ordered his three remaining companies to hold the line Ash Crater – Zambuk Track – Ultimo Crater (where the battalion was in touch with the South Staffords) and thence down to the edge of the wood. Repeated attacks were also made on this line throughout the rest of the day, but it was still intact by nightfall. A request was made for the reserve 10/Cheshires to send a company to link up between the Wiltshires and whatever was left of 75 Brigade, but that battalion appears to have already been sent by brigade in the other direction, towards the left flank and the Douve (none of which is mentioned in the Cheshires or brigade war diary). During the hours of darkness, contact was established on the right with 2/South Lancashire and with elements of the 25th Machine Gun Battalion, making a reasonably continuous line to face the dawn. With his battalion reduced by the fighting of 10 April down to about 130 officers and men in all, and with his headquarters now practically being in the new front line, Ogilvie moved rearwards to the Catacombs, a location which had the advantage of a deep-buried signal cable line by which contact could be made with division and the artillery. During the night a welcome draft of thirty men arrived.

In the early morning of 11 April, Ogilvie was hit by a bombshell of news: he was told that there was now a gap of some two miles on his right, as 75 Brigade had carried out a deep withdrawal, leaving the battalions of 7 Brigade in an uncomfortable, exposed salient. The area of Hill 63 and the Catacombs came under heavy and sustained German shellfire during the morning, but despite frantic SOS signals from the front line and calls put through the telephone system, the British artillery response was weak and made little difference to the growing pressure from German infantry. After conferring with Lieutenant Colonel Finch of the 4/South Staffords and hearing reports that the enemy was in occupation of Grande and Petit Munque Farms, further bad news came when brigade told Ogilvie that it was imperative to hold on to St Yves and Hill 63, and that he should 'hold on to the last and then fight my way back'.

At 6pm, a fresh bombardment heralded a strong German infantry attack from Ploegsteert Wood and up the steep-sided Hill 63. Intense Lewis gun and rifle fire was opened upon the advancing infantry, but the hill was soon surrounded from the rear and with it fell the entrances to the Catacombs. Within half an hour, Ogilvie – wounded in the ear – fell into captivity, along with others of his headquarters. About forty-five of the Wiltshires, led by Captain Geoffrey Wait, managed to escape from the forward position and through St Yves before the German net was fully closed around them. What was left of 4/South Staffords also escaped, moving rearwards towards Neuve Église, as did the 10/Cheshires. The 4/King's Shropshire Light Infantry of 56th Brigade, which had been held in reserve on the rear face of Hill 63 and at Underhill Farm, covered their retreat until it too was ordered to withdraw west. By 5am on 12 April, the remnants of the brigade were gathered in a position near Aux Trois Rois Cabaret, west of Neuve Église.

Divisional artillery, medical, engineers and transport.
The 25th Division's own artillery was not present at the outset of the battle, for it was still on the road from the Somme. On 10 April, the division took over 'Tovey's Group, consisting of the 11th and 2nd New Zealand Army Brigades. These were normal brigades of field artillery, but not under the permanent orders of any given division, instead coming directly under Army control: this was a development of 1917 that had already proved most successful, providing greater flexibility in massing artillery resources where they were most needed. At around 10am the artillery brigades were instructed to act independently as far as any withdrawal was concerned and to engage the enemy wherever he could be seen; 41 Brigade of the heavy Royal Garrison Artillery also came under divisional control at this time. The day proved to be a hard one for these various units.

The officers and men of 2 NZ Army Brigade had only arrived in the area on 7 April, having recently been at Ypres, where it had suffered numerous casualties. The brigade was comprised of numbers 2, 5, 6 (Howitzer) and 9 Batteries, and was temporarily grouped together with 84 and 85 Batteries of 11 Army Brigade RFA to cover the whole front from Warneton down to Deûlémont.

The batteries, which were arrayed along both sides of the Ypres-Armentières road north of Hyde Park Corner, came under fire as soon as the German bombardment began, and very soon opened counter-preparation fire on positions where it was believed enemy infantry would mass for an attack. Once information came that the Germans were advancing, the guns shortened their range and continued in action: but information was hard to come by, and the brigade was soon in no doubt as to why:

'Serious and unnecessary trouble arose at the outset, when signal personnel manning various Corps exchanges were found to have decamped, apparently on the first news of the enemy advance – thus denying to regimental troops their reliance on buried and air lines when they were most required. It was a common experience both to find these exchanges empty and secondly, after communication was established, for the exchange to evacuate without warning.'

(War Diary, IX Corps, Commander Royal Artillery)

Even with the signals problems, it was soon evident to the New Zealanders that the enemy was making fast progress and at 6am the brigade was ordered to withdraw towards Wulverghem. Little difficulty was encountered by the three 18-pounder batteries (although their movement left a period when the poor infantry of the division was provided with little field artillery support). They were in action again by 11.30am and fired on enemy targets in the Ploegsteert area throughout the rest of the day and evening. At about 8pm the brigade was ordered to withdraw further westwards, as the enemy was believed to be in area of Hill 63 and at Grande Munque Farm. The larger howitzers of 6 Battery could not be as quickly moved from their pits, and instead the gun teams were ordered to fire to the last round and only bring away the sights and breech blocks at the last possible moment. The battery fought on until about noon, by which time its ammunition was exhausted and the gunners began move. On the day the brigade suffered casualties of nine killed and twenty-nine wounded, whilst one man, Gunner 18236 Llewellyn Gwilliam, fell into German hands.

84 Battery, nominally of 11 Army Brigade RFA but temporarily grouped with the New Zealanders, fought on until surrounded early in morning. Having fired all of their supply of ammunition, the men blew up the guns and got away, covering their own withdrawal with Lewis gun fire. The battery's Bombardier 800999 Sidney Morris, who was awarded the Military Medal for his exploits on the day, wrote: 'Our [signal, telephone] wires had all gone when the shelling had been on [for] minutes. I and two of my men worked on the wires for three hours, until the enemy were seen advancing. Several of our men were captured, but I was a sprinter – at least, I was at that time – and a good one too.' 85 Battery, located at Hill 63, remained in action until getting away safely about 5pm.

The other two batteries of 11 Army Brigade were positioned south west of Ploegsteert, supporting 75 Brigade. They came under enemy machine gun fire by 7.30am. 83 Battery had to abandon four of its 18-

pounder guns and D/11 two of its howitzers. The remainder came back into action near Petit-Pont, south east of Neuve Église, by about 10am. The four batteries fired some 6500 rounds during the day.

Before the German attack began, the medical facilities had been established in locations suited to the normal trench warfare that had been going on in this area since 1914. 75 Field Ambulance set up its Advanced Dressing Station at Underhill Farm, in the lee of Hill 63, for casualties from 7 Brigade; 77 Field Ambulance established one at the Brewery (north of Chapelle Rompue, on the outskirts of Le Bizet) for 75 Brigade. Most casualties would then go rearwards to the Divisional Main Dressing Station at Pont d'Achelles. All of these locations came under fire in the early hours, and during the day a gradual withdrawal was made in which the MDS was relocated as far away as Outtersteene. Underhill Farm was evacuated as early as 9.30am, save for the stretcher bearer parties, who continued to bring wounded men in from Hyde Park Corner for several hours.

The 25th Division's Machine Gun Battalion had relieved three companies of 2nd Australian Machine Gun Battalion on 1-2 April, taking over their posts. As with all units of its division, it had suffered serious losses in the 'Michael' fighting and received draft of eleven officers and 260 men after it had moved to Flanders. Half (eight guns and teams) of its reserve B Company had been sent to join 74 Brigade heading for Croix du Bac during 9 April. The guns in the posts opened fire on pre-planned SOS lines at 6am, but very soon heard that enemy had already got through to the support lines. From this point onwards there is no coherent narrative, for the battalion did not work as a unit. Its guns fought essentially independently for next three days. It is, however, clear that battalion headquarters and some 250 men under Lieutenant Colonel John Deane-Drummond moved to hold the de Seule – Red Lodge road, and that later in the day (at 4.30pm) he led a counter-attack. Armed with rifles, and together with 2/South Lancashire, this detachment worked to clear Germans from houses along the Ploegsteert-Romarin road. Deane-Drummond was wounded in the arm in the process; Major Ashcroft took command of the battalion.

The story of the rest of the morning and afternoon is one of improvised attempts to organise a force to hold the enemy, but was ultimately one of defeat and withdrawal. By 9.15am, a typically scratch force of half of 2/South Lancashire, the remnants of the 11/Cheshires, 200 men of 134 Army Troops Company and the 1st Australian Army Troops Company of the Royal Engineers were digging in and forming a line across the roads leading to Romarin and Le Bizet. The force held on, adjusting its position, under repeated attack for several hours.

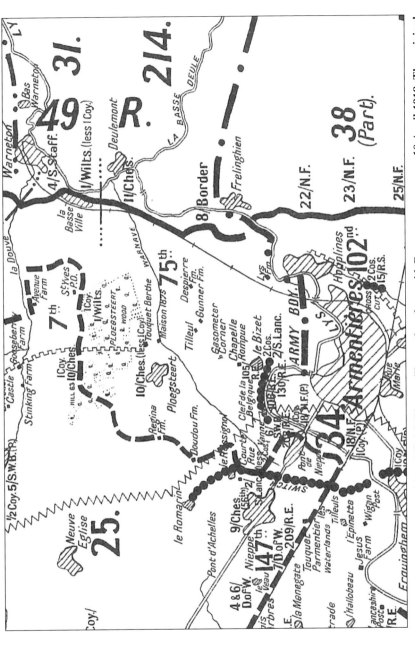

Part of a map from the British Official History, illustrating the rapid German progress on 10 April 1918. The original British front is solid black and the dashed line represents its position at day's end.

The 34th Division and the Armentières flank.

The 34th Division had been withdrawn from the Somme fighting and arrived on the Lys on 28 March, with the exception of its own artillery. It took temporary ownership of the artillery of the 38th (Welsh) Division. By 9 April the division was holding a stretch of the front line, but only its left half was in the geographic area of this book. This was held by 102 Brigade. It is, however, important to understand what had happened on the division's right. The German attack on 9 April broke through the 40th Division, and while the main body pushed directly northwards towards the Lys, elements also wheeled to their right, threatening the right flank of the 34th Division and potentially cutting its men off in Armentières. Gradually, units of the division formed a flank defence that held intact; by day's end this flank had stretched up to Erquinghem-Lys. German progress on 10 April, in which they broke through the 25th Division's front at Ploegsteert, left the 34th Division in an increasingly precarious position.

By 7.15am, the German advance against 8/Border (75 Brigade) had reached Lys Farm, which was across the river from, but some way behind, the immediate left of the 34th Division's line. This sector was being held by 102 Brigade, which had placed 22/Northumberland Fusiliers next to the Borders. This battalion was not directly attacked but was in danger of being cut off should the enemy advance any deeper. Divisional HQ ordered artillery and machine gun fire to be directed against the enemy, but otherwise it was not itself attacked.

At 10am, IX Corps ordered the 34th Division to carry out the most difficult task of withdrawing from its front, passing through gas-soaked and under-fire Armentières. With the battalions leaving outposts to act as rearguards to cover the withdrawal, this movement was to commence at 3pm. 102 Brigade was to take up a new line on the northern bank of the Lys, stretching from La Clef de la Belgique down to just south of the railway line near Pont de Nieppe. The divisional Royal Engineers were ordered to place a demolition party at each bridge over the Lys and to destroy them once British forces were across; the same applied to the pioneers of 18/Northumberland Fusiliers in charge of the many cork and plank bridges.

The left-most unit of the 34th Division, 22/Northumberland Fusiliers, reported that enemy shell fire increased as they began to slip away, but the men escaped through Armentières with remarkably few casualties. The battalion's war diary assigns this in part to the fact that they were not harassed by low-flying aeroplanes: we can only imagine what effect that such aircraft might have had, as the battalion moved along the built-up Nouvel Houplines-Armentières road. The battalion came under machine

38

The 34th Division took up positions along the Lys at Pont de Nieppe, the first – if weak - prepared defensive line west of Armentières. (Author)

gun fire from the south (that is, from German troops in the area of Erquinghem-Lys) as they tried to take up their allotted position along the river in front of Pont de Nieppe.

Withdrawing behind the 22nd came 23/Northumberland Fusiliers, who had been holding the front line east of Houplines and Nouvel Houplines. They too managed to reach their allotted line without too much difficulty, except from machine gun fire as they came into line south of the 22nd; they occupied Burnley and Manchester Posts.

South of Armentières, the units of the division's 103 Brigade crossed the Lys by the railway bridge near the large jute factory, while 101 Brigade mainly used an emergency bridge somewhat closer to the enemy that by now was in Erquinghem-Lys. The sappers did their work and the many bridges were destroyed; the Germans would have to go around Armentières if they were to make progress – but by nightfall they were doing exactly that.

During the night of 9-10 April, 147 Brigade had arrived from the 49th (West Riding) Division and sent its 1/4 Duke of Wellington's (West Riding Regiment) forwards to Erquinghem-Lys. It encountered large numbers of British troops, mainly of the broken 40th Division, coming the other way before it reached the village. Battalion headquarters was set up in Wigan Post on the north bank of the Lys, and it then sent its companies across the river to assist the hard-pressed 103 and 101

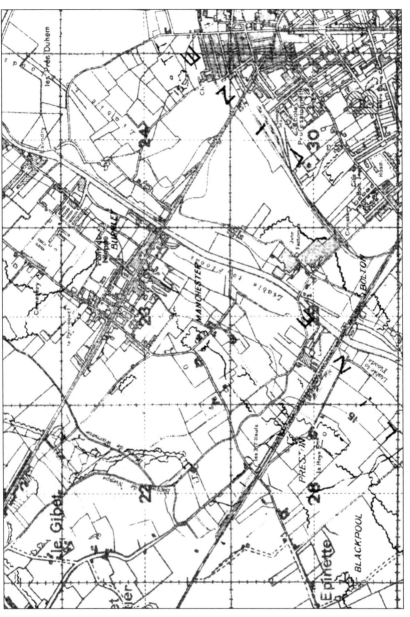

As the 34th Division withdrew from Armentières, battalions of the Northumberland Fusiliers occupied posts that had been constructed at Pont de Nieppe, on the far side of the Lys.

Brigades. They met no enemy directly, but the battalion suffered casualties from heavy shell and machine-gun fire as it deployed along the *Rue du Moulin*, facing towards Fort Rompu. A German attack was beaten off; large numbers of battlefield stragglers continued to come in from the south, and the scene was one of utmost danger and uncertainty. During the afternoon, the battalion and rest of the brigade were ordered to withdraw across the river in the direction of Nieppe, where it came into position as a reserve behind the three brigades of the 34th Division that were now lining the river bank.

While the division's withdrawal was underway, the German *Sixth Army* had made further progress in its southern attack. It was reportedly on the Armentières-Bailleul railway line between Trois Arbres and Steenwerck Station; well behind the line to which 102 Brigade had been ordered, and had crossed that railway at Le Veau at the very time the withdrawal began. There are some sadly ill-documented accounts of a local counter-attack by cooks, transport men and details of the 34th Division, driving back this incursion at Le Veau. Even so, this threat caused the division to re-align part of its new front, with 101 and 103 Brigades swinging their right to hold the railway as a flank defence. They were in position by 5am on 11 April.

It proved to be a rather quieter night, during which many stragglers passed though the divisional area. The brigades held on through 11 April under intense shelling and repeated efforts to attack, although these appear to be piecemeal rather than a concerted effort. The most serious periods came at 9.10am, when German forces attacked 102 Brigade from their north and south, and at 11.50am, when 23/Northumberland Fusiliers were forced out of Burnley Post at Pont de Nieppe.

Ominous reports began to come in at about noon that the 25th Division, which had been standing on the Lys on the 34th Division's left, was now under attack and being pushed rearwards. An enemy advance there would post a considerable threat to the 34th Division, which was also hemmed in on its southern flank. Arrangements were made for 88 Brigade of the 29th Division (most of which was now further west and out of the geographic scope of this volume) to form a defensive line across the Bailleul road behind the 34th Division, and to hold it at all costs; and for a hastily-assembled composite battalion (including, at least, elements of the Yorkshire and Middlesex Regiments of the 40th

88 Brigade was commanded by Brigadier General Bernard Freyberg, already famous for his exploits at Gallipoli and a VC from the Somme in late 1916. (Author)

Division, the 15/Royal Scots and a company of 18/Northumberland Fusiliers) to assist the 25th Division by carrying out a counter-attack east of Papot.

There was a fleeting but extraordinary opportunity for German gunners, had they but known it, when during the afternoon all five brigadiers (of the 34th Division and 88 and 147 Brigades) gathered together at Papot Mill to agree the detail of a plan to withdraw towards Bailleul. It would be another operation of extreme difficulty, for the enemy was holding the area of Steenwerck and Trois Arbres on the west flank of the withdrawal, although Divisional HQ received information that the British 31st Division, not too far away to the west of Steenwerck, was about to make a counter-attack. The units were told that they might have to fight their way through to the rear. That the withdrawal was completed without significant disruption during the evening may be due in part to the effect of the 31st Division's attack. By nightfall, the three brigades of the 34th Division had made it as far as La Crèche and were on the start of a gradual rise in the ground toward the hills in front of Bailleul: they had encountered a few German machine gun patrols in the area into which they were withdrawing, but these were dealt with and some prisoners taken. That done, the battalions received their first rations for three days.

Von Eberhardt's X Reserve Corps **quickly pushed through Ploegsteert and on towards Nieppe. (Author)**

Casualty Clearing Stations.
There were fifteen Casualty Clearing Stations (CCS) located within Second Army's area, of which seven were located within nine miles of the original front line and the others further to the rear. The German advance soon threatened these units, and while none were located on ground which the Germans eventually captured, several of them were close enough to be at serious risk of long-range artillery fire. All of the seven located closest to the front line moved during the battle: the first to go was 11 CCS, which vacated Godewaersvelde and moved to Blendecques on 13 April (mainly due to the threat from the direction of Méteren); next day, 10 and 3 CCS left Rémy Siding (Lijssenthoek) and Nine Elms (near Poperinge) for Arnéke and Esquelbecq. The latter place received 2 Canadian CCS from Rémy Siding on 15 April. Finally, as the battle pressed on in the Kemmel area later in the month, the group of 30,

62 and 64 CCS all went to Watten, having left Roesbrugge, Mendinghem and Bandaghem (the latter two names were made up by some wag of the BEF, along with a CCS at 'Dozinghem') respectively.

Moving a CCS was not a matter to be undertaken lightly, for it usually comprised a mixture of huts and tents for wards, surgical units and accommodation, and all the equipment of a hospital of considerable size. Inevitably, if it became necessary to move, then a speedy return to work was desirable. Despite the evident disruption and effort, the medical service was maintained throughout and no stations reported any significant problems in terms of processing casualties.

Chapter Four

The Attack on Messines Ridge

North of the River Douve, the British front was held by the 19th (Western) Division. It had arrived only a few days before the battle and had been sent to this area in the belief that it was likely to remain quiet, giving the division an opportunity to rebuild after being severely handled in Operation Michael. All its battalions reported the situation quiet on their front on 9 April, although the sound of heavy gunfire was heard to the south in 25th Division's area and beyond. The 19th Division was holding a front line of some six kilometres in length, stretching from the Douve up to Charity Farm, east of Ravine Wood. It had two brigades in line, separated by the little Wambeke stream.

Facing the division's right-hand sector, *226 Infanterie-Regiment* of *49th Reserve-Division* was positioned on the north bank of the Douve. To its north came *17th Reserve-Division*, which had placed the Schleswig-Holstein *163 Infanterie-Regiment* facing Gapaard and the Lubeck *162 Infanterie-Regiment* facing Messines.

The front line from which the German attack began was where they had managed finally to hold the successful British attack of the Battle of Messines in June 1917. It faced a gradual slope up to the line of the ridge that runs south from Ypres, through the large villages of Wytschaete and Messines. Beyond the ridge to the west, the ground falls slowly away before eventually rising again, initially to higher ground and on which sits Neuve Église. Most of the ground that the advancing infantry would need to cross was already devastated from previous fighting and the merciless artillery bombardments of 1917:

Sieger's XVIII Corps attacked in the area north of the River Douve, making progress against Messines but finding Wytschaete a much harder proposition. (Author)

shell-cratered, riddled with barbed wire, pillboxes, trench railways, dugouts and tunnels, battlefield cemeteries – and several vast craters (already becoming pools) that resulted from underground mines that were blown on 7 June 1917.

Messines, in better times easily visible from all directions from its elevated position and characteristic church tower, was now little more than a tortured pile of rubble and a rabbit-warren of dugouts. It represented a physical challenge to infantrymen of both sides and particularly to the German technical, transport and supply troops, who would need to cross and bridge this ground. The British also faced a challenge, for their front line posts were inevitably situated on open ground and a forward slope: they were readily visible to German observers. The British artillery could at least take advantage of a position on the rear (western) side of the ridge line in order to be out of direct sight; but in reality and with aerial observation, there was no hiding place.

South of the Wambeke, Brigadier General Thomas Cubitt's 57 Brigade had all three of its battalions along its 3400m front line and would rely on the division's reserves should it need rapid support. Cubitt was a gunner and a 'fire-eater with a marvellous flow of language', who placed his 8/Gloucesters on the right, 10/Worcesters in the centre and 10/Royal Warwicks on the left. The brigade had been in this position for eight days when the German attack struck; it was tired and due for relief. North of Cubitt's men came 58 Brigade under Brigadier General Alfred Glasgow, holding a somewhat shorter line, with the 6/Wiltshires on the right and 9/Royal Welsh Fusiliers to their left. The two met at Junction Buildings, south of Green Wood. North of the Fusiliers came the operational boundary with the 9th (Scottish) Division. The brigade's third battalion, 9/Welsh, was in support. A total of thirty-four guns of the divisional 19th Machine Gun Battalion were deployed to support these units, leaving another thirty in reserve near Neuve Église.

Both brigades occupied a discontinuous 'front line', consisting of three lines of posts. Work was being carried out on a reserve line, with the intention of making another chain of posts into a continuous defence, but this was nowhere near complete by 10 April. Finally, a notional 'Corps Line' of posts ran parallel to and east of the ridge. The deployment of the Wiltshires is instructive: two companies (A and B) held the forward chains of posts, while two others (C and D) were fully two kilometres behind them, in the reserve line. The 9/Royal Welsh Fusiliers were similarly arranged, with their A and D Companies in the posts.

57 Brigade.
When the German artillery switched its bombardment to the front line posts, reported by division to have taken place at 5.30am, it fell most heavily on 57 Brigade and particularly on its centre and right battalions. When the subsequent infantry attack came in behind a creeping barrage at 6am, it too was focused on 57 Brigade. The fog, speed of advance and sheer weight of numbers saw the Germans quickly penetrating the gaps between the brigade's posts. It was later calculated that eleven German

45

battalions and two storm troop units attacked the brigade's three battalions. Very soon the Gloucesters and Worcesters were reporting that the enemy had got in between them and were enveloping the posts from the rear. They received no response from the artillery, even after sending up SOS flares: it is possible that in the early morning gloom they were simply not seen. The 10/Warwicks, finding that the enemy were breaking through the Worcesters, were forced to retire: not westwards on their own reserve line but in a northwards direction towards Wytschaete and 58 Brigade. C and D Companies, the reserve of the 6/Wiltshires, moved to man a long, duck-boarded but shallow and partly flooded communication trench, Manchester Street, and eventually connected with the Warwicks.

At much the same time, 7 Brigade, south and across the Douve, sent up an SOS, too: no significant help was likely to come from that direction and it became quite clear to 57 Brigade that German troops were advancing from 7 Brigade's sector at Warneton, up the Hirondelle Road onto the rising ground at Gapaard. The forward posts were very quickly eliminated, and the brigade's war diary uses unusually candid language to describe the scene.

'Practically none of the garrisons were ever seen again and in one case the enemy were seen all around a British post killing off the garrison, who were greatly hampered in their defence by the large camouflage screens which were pulled over the posts at daybreak each day to protect them from the enemy's air observation.'

By 6.40am, all of 57 Brigade's front and support positions had fallen, and the three battalions had all suffered heavy losses. The brigade's Trench Mortar Battery lost all the guns that had been in the forward area, and over fifty percent of its personnel. The Germans moved on to begin to attack the elements in the reserve line.

With its 56 Brigade having now been moved to assist the defence of the 25th and 34th Divisions, the 19th Division took steps to order its only reserves to hand, 81 and 82 Field Companies RE and two companies of the pioneers, 5/South Wales Borderers, to hold the 'Corps Line'. Permission was also obtained from IX Corps for two companies of 8/North Staffordshires to be released from 56 Brigade in order to assist: they began to move forwards from Wulverghem.

By 8.30am the German attack had also broken the 'Corps Line' and was swarming through Messines. Three battalions of *162 and 163 Infanterie-Regiments* reached the western outskirts, having completed an advance of three kilometres, and put out a left flank defence facing the Douve and blocking any would-be incursion towards Bethleem Farm.

Many men of the 19th (Western) Division died while holding exposed posts on the gentle eastern slopes of Messines Ridge. (Brett Butterworth)

Half a battalion of the North Staffords was ordered to recapture the town. In its attempt to advance, the battalion reached a line through the hospice grounds and held on under fire. During the day it lost five officers and 150 men killed or wounded; the two officers who lost their lives were notable characters. Captain Wilfrid Meir, who commanded B Company, came from Longdon in Staffordshire. In 1914 he had been named as the Manchester University's best student in science, awarded the Beyer Fellowship, and had a Master's degree. Meir's grave is visited in one of the battlefield tours in this book. His brother Gilbert was killed on 1 July 1916. The more junior officer to die, Second Lieutenant Christopher Lucas, was the grandson of Birmingham electrical engineering entrepreneur Joseph Lucas. Known to his family as 'Hollie' after his middle name of Hollins, he has no known grave and is commemorated on the Tyne Cot Memorial. In the King's Heath area of Birmingham, where his parents lived, Hollie Lucas Road was named after him, as was a small park nearby.

The situation was most obscure on the division's front for much of the morning, but by 9am it appeared to 58 Brigade that the nearest troops of 57 Brigade were a few of the 10/Warwicks holding a line at Pick

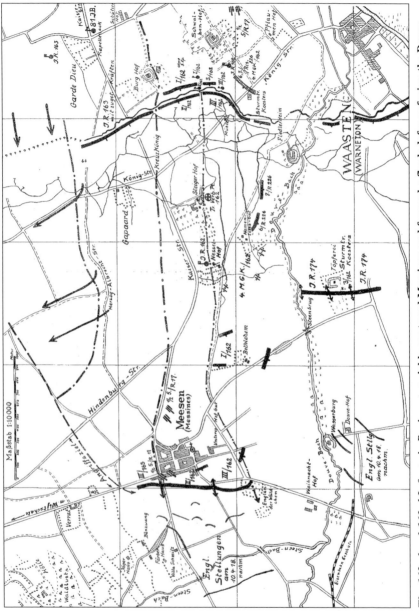

The *162nd* and *163rd Infanterie-Regiments* quickly captured Messines and formed a flank defence facing the Douve.

Messines was destroyed during the fighting of June 1917: the Germans had to advance through a vast field of rubble. (Author)

House. These men had been with battalion headquarters: its war diary says there were about a hundred men in all, and others were at Lumm Farm. The Warwicks gained touch with the 6/Wiltshire on their left but found nothing on their right: later reports suggest that there were about fifty leaderless men of the 10/Worcesters between Pick House and Messines.

Captain Eric Dougall ran the guns of his battery to fire over open sights at close range at advancing enemy. (Author)

At this point, an act of heroism by a gunner officer and his men rallied the infantry in a very uncertain situation that might well have deteriorated into a rout. A Battery of 88 Brigade of the Royal Field Artillery had been in action on the reverse slope southwest of Pick House. On moving his 18-pounder guns forward in order to find a better firing location, Captain Eric Dougall MC, sensing the desperation around him, halted, and ordered his guns to fire in close-range support to the infantry. Men of the Worcesters rallied around the battery, taking cover in trenches around it. The guns became an epicentre of resistance, although swept by machine gun and rifle fire. The fog became its salvation as German guns could not easily range onto it. The eloquent citation of Dougall's posthumous Victoria Cross tells the story:

49

'For most conspicuous bravery and skilful leadership in the field when in command of his battery. Capt. Dougall maintained his guns in action from early morning throughout a heavy concentration of gas and high-explosive shell fire. Finding that he could not clear the crest owing to the withdrawal of our line, Captain Dougall ran his guns on to the top of the ridge to fire over open sights. By this time our infantry had been pressed back in line with the guns. Captain Dougall at once assumed command of the situation, rallied and organised the infantry, supplied them with Lewis guns, and armed as many gunners as he could spare with rifles. With these he formed a line in front of his battery which during this period was harassing the advancing enemy with a rapid rate of fire. Although exposed to both rifle and machine gun fire, this officer fearlessly walked about as though on parade, calmly giving orders and encouraging everybody. He inspired the infantry with his assurance that, 'So long as you stick to your trenches I will keep my guns here'. This line was maintained throughout the day, thereby delaying the enemy's advance for over twelve hours. In the evening, having expended all ammunition, the battery received orders to withdraw. This was done by man-handling the guns over a distance of about 800 yards of shell-cratered country, an almost impossible feat considering the ground and the intense machine gun fire. Owing to Captain Dougall's personality and skilful leadership throughout this trying day there is no doubt that a serious breach in our line was averted. This gallant officer was killed four days later whilst directing the fire of his battery.' Eric Dougall lies in Westoutre British Cemetery.

By 10am the North Staffs had made good headway in the face of strong opposition and had reached the western edge of Messines, even taking some prisoners, although the definite situation was not known at brigade headquarters until 11.35am. The 81 Field Company RE and South Wales Borderers had also succeeded in occupying the 'Corps Line' as ordered. In the afternoon, the North Staffs pushed on and recapture Swayne's Farm and stretched out leftwards to join up with the Warwicks at Pick House. That battalion's headquarters had been forced by shellfire to retire past Wytschaete to North House, but a detachment remained in trenches west of Pick House until it too was compelled to move.

With the Germans having gained the tactical advantage of being on the high ground, the 19th (Western) Division desperately attempted to organise a new reserve line on the western slope of the ridge. It was proposed to run from Maedelstede Farm, to the east of Spanbroekmolen, to In de Kruisstraat Cabaret, and on to Bristol Castle. It was manned by the last two companies of the 8/North Staffs, having latterly been released by Corps, joined by around 700 surplus personnel and drafts that had just arrived in the area from England and twelve of the machine gun teams that had been held in reserve. This improvised force was organised by Lieutenant Colonel Ralph Umfreville of the 8/Gloucesters.

At 12.25pm the South African Brigade was transferred to the 19th Division's control from its parent, the 9th (Scottish) Division. It was assigned to 57 Brigade, with the intention of using it to counter-attack and recapture Messines. But it was a shadow of the formation best known for its fights at Delville Wood in 1916 and more recently at Marrières Wood in Operation 'Michael'. Now it was a brigade in name only, having sustained sixty percent casualties during late March and with no immediate prospect of reinforcement, the 1512 officers and men that remained amounted to little more than an oversized battalion. As such it was not considered fit to hold a normal brigade line and there were discussions about whether to restructure it into one battalion or two. The South Africans were commanded by Somme veteran Brigadier General William Tanner, who had recently taken the place of his captured predecessor, and now comprised the 1st, 2nd and 4th South African Infantry Battalions. On their approach march from La Clytte they encountered a steady and pitiable stream of civilian refugees fleeing the battle area.

The brigade was ordered to advance in the area between Messines and Lumm Farm: first to reach the ridge road; then the reserve line between Bethleem Farm and Pick House (meaning that it needed to go through the devastated village); and go on from there onto the downward eastern slope. Deploying into attack position at 5.45pm, 1/SAI was to advance on Messines, with 2/SAI on its left, aiming at the Pick House area. 4/SAI, the Transvaal Scottish, was held in support but lent a company to the attack on Messines.

The regiment's story was later written by eminent author John Buchan, later ennobled as Viscount Tweedsmuir and who became Governor General of Canada:

'In the mist it was not easy to keep close touch, and 1/SAI reached the western slopes ahead of the time, so that for a little its left flank was out of touch with 2/SAI. As had been expected, our artillery support proved very weak, and in no way affected the German machine gunners established in our old strong-points and their snipers in shell holes. As the South Africans approached the crest they were met by a heavy fire from the outskirts of the village, and from Middle Farm, Four Huns Farm, and Pick House.

Nevertheless, by 6.30pm 2/SAI had won its first objective and crossed the Messines-Wytschaete road. Presently it had reached the second position, D Company, on the left, capturing Lumm Farm with two machine guns, much ammunition, and part of the garrison, while the right companies, reinforced by part of 4/SAI, took Four Huns Farm, Middle Farm, and Swayne's Farm, together with four machine guns and many prisoners. Pick House itself, however, which consisted of three concrete pill-boxes, was too strongly held, and Captain Jacobs, commanding 2/SAI, was compelled to swing back his left company to Earl Farm, where it formed a defensive flank in touch with 5/South Wales Borderers in 58th Brigade. Here it was heavily enfiladed from a strong-point north of Messines and from Pick House, and early in the night Jacobs took up a crescent-shaped line astride the Messines-Wytschaete road, with his right resting on Middle Farm, his left on Petits Puits, and his own headquarters at Hell Farm. His casualties on the left had been slight, but the companies of 2/SAI on the right had lost some fifty per cent of their effectives ...

In the meantime 1/SAI Regiment had met the enemy issuing from Messines, had charged him with the bayonet, and had driven him back well over the ridge. In the eastern outskirts of the village, however, they were held up by heavy machine-gun fire from the direction of Bethlehem [sic] Farm, and from various strong-points north of it. One of the latter was captured, and many prisoners were taken. For an hour there was severe hand-to-hand fighting, in which many casualties were sustained, all the officers in the vicinity being either killed or wounded.

Captain Burgess gallantly led a small detachment through heavy fire to the east of the village. Owing to the shortage of men the position soon became untenable, and what was left of 1/SAI was compelled to withdraw to a line about a hundred yards west of Messines [effectively reinforcing the 8/North Staffords].'

Ultimately, this meant that Messines had been lost to British arms by nightfall. After the enormous efforts of previous years to capture this ground, this was indeed a most significant blow. When taken in concert with the German progress at Ploegsteert, the way was open for a further advance to the next high ground: Neuve Église. But if British forces could keep hold of that part of Messines Ridge that runs up through Wytschaete to St. Eloi, any deeper German advance would be endangered by enfilading fire. It was a very big 'if'. The question by the end of 10 April 1918 was: could they?

58 Brigade

Although it came under ceaseless shellfire during the morning, to which was added much machine gun fire as the Germans got up onto the higher ground of the Gapaard spur, the 6/Wiltshires did not come under a major infantry attack for much of the day but later had a very torrid few hours. The battalion had to adjust on its right, to keep in touch with the 10/Warwicks once it was appreciated that the latter was being pushed back to and then from Pick House. At 3.30pm, the battalion opened fire on German troops that could be seen massing ready to advance, and appear to have broken the attack up.

On their left, between Junction Buildings and Charity Farm, the 9/Welsh Fusiliers reported at noon that their front line posts had been overwhelmed. They had come under an exceedingly heavy and accurate artillery bombardment, particularly around Ravine Wood. The forward posts were 'all blown in', leaving a gap which German infantry soon penetrated. Support posts in Rose Wood were evacuated at about 3pm, at which point touch was lost with the 6/Wiltshires and the brigade's defence became fragmented.

At 4.30pm, brigade ordered the battalions to evacuate their posts and withdraw. Within an hour, German troops had advanced to occupy the original British front and prepared to press on. At much the same time that the South Africans were counter-attacking not far away at Messines, at 6pm both flanks of the 6/Wiltshires, now near Oosttaverne, gave way under heavy attack. Desperate orders for a withdrawal to the reserve line did not reach their two companies holding the support trenches, and few of those men ever returned. Among them was Major H. Wilfred House:

'As darkness began to fall I had to decide what we would do. I had become convinced that battalion HQ couldn't reach us and therefore we were almost completely, if not completely, isolated. I had about 25 or 30 men with me and whenever we tried to move in the direction of what we thought might be our own lines we were heavily fired at and as darkness come on we could see by the Very lights that the Germans had got some way behind us. I collected our little party and told them what I though the position was and that I saw little hope of cutting our way out and therefore it seemed to me that the only thing was to form ourselves into groups of 2 or 3 men each and try to make our way through in the dark. I could only tell them what I believed to be the direction of the British line and advise them to watch the Very lights which would confirm that they were moving in the right direction. I decided that the best thing would be for parties of 2 or 3 men who

53

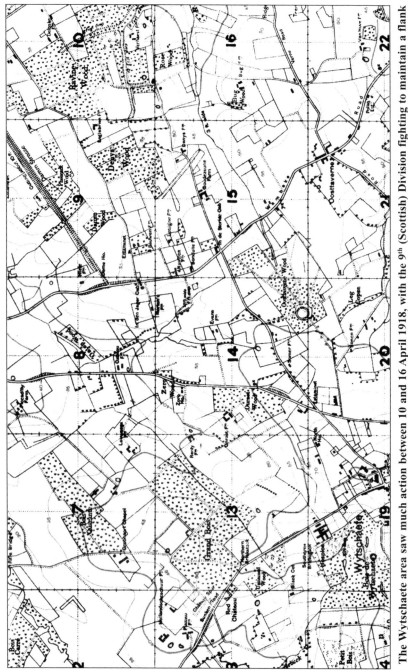

The Wytschaete area saw much action between 10 and 16 April 1918, with the 9th (Scottish) Division fighting to maintain a flank protecting Ypres.

were friends to work together and I arranged that I would move off with a young officer called Findlay and that we would set off as soon as it was really dark. We didn't know the ground very well as we had only gone into the line the day before and had never been as far forward as that before, but I had an idea that I knew roughly that there was a stream running at right angles to what had been our original line and Findlay and I decided that we would make for the water and walk in it as being less likely to meet parties of Germans.'

Moving in the direction of Very light flares, House and Findlay followed the line of the stream (almost certainly the Rozebeek) and eventually took cover when they heard foreign conversation ahead. We can only imagine their relief on finding that the voices were of native speakers from the Welsh battalions of their brigade. House also recalled how in the early part of the night enemy shells were falling 1000 yards *behind* their most advanced troops – clearly the Germans were struggling with battlefield communication quite as much as the British.

Despite the evidently hopeless situation, House's comrade Captain George Kent simply refused to retire without orders. His company was killed or captured to a man: unlike the pragmatic House who lived to fight another day, Kent spent the rest of the war in captivity.

With the enemy pressing, battalion headquarters joined in the defence of its right flank: in this action, its commanding officer, Lieutenant Colonel George Monreal, and his second in command, Major Alan Garthwaite, were both wounded. Monreal, a native of Malta, who also had connections in South Africa and could speak six languages, succumbed to his wounds next day; he lies in Locre Hospice Cemetery.

About 7.30pm the Signals Sergeant of the battalion reached 58 Brigade's HQ, reporting that his battalion's headquarters had been driven out of its dugout and surrounded by enemy troops who had advanced from the direction of Torreken Farm. The battalion was to all intents and purposes destroyed. Only a detachment of about fifty men managed to move northward and link up with the 9/Welsh; these aside, handfuls of isolated men, numbering about seventy-five in all, reached British lines after nightfall.

The elements of 9/Welsh Fusiliers who had managed to withdraw took up a position in the reserve line and held on until about 7pm, when it was realised that Germans had broken through the Wiltshires and were now behind them in Oosttaverne Wood. The battalion was now in serious trouble. Its right company, D, was soon surrounded and fought almost to the last; only about twenty men of the company managed to survive the battle. There were also concerns about C Company, which was last heard of in the reserve line at Goudezeune Farm, but it transpired that this unit held on in position until its survivors began to withdraw to safety in the early hours of 11 April.

North of the Royal Welsh Fusiliers, the 9th (Scottish) Division had no hard information about what was happening. A platoon was sent out at 4pm under Lieutenant John Robertson of the 8/Black Watch, ordered to patrol through Oosttaverne Wood to try to ascertain the situation. He came across the battalion headquarters of the 9/Welsh Fusiliers on the eastern edge of the wood at about 5.30pm, discovering that its commanding officer, Major H Lloyd Williams, had no reliable information about the location or status of his forward companies. Deciding to go on and see for himself,

'I continued through Denys Wood to the Dammstrasse and saw not more than 20 men of 58th Brigade scattered along this line [including some in Goudezeune Farm, possibly the Fusiliers C Company]. We saw Germans about 500 yards away … As it was getting dark I commenced to return, intending to revisit the battalion HQ of the Royal Welsh Fusiliers. On approaching the north side of Oosttaverne Wood I met the Medical Officer of the Fusiliers, who informed me that the Germans were in the wood and had captured all the officers of the battalion's headquarters. I was never more surprised in my life.'

At 10.30pm the situation of 58 Brigade's front was that the 9/Welsh were holding the cutting south and east of Wytschaete and a company was holding a position near Pheasant Wood. Part of one of its companies was attached to the 6/Wiltshires, supposedly at Gun Farm – but nothing had been heard of them and they were evidently cut off by the German advance. Of the 9/Welsh Fusiliers, even less was known by brigade headquarters, except that its fourth company was in reserve at Denys Wood.

The 9th (Scottish) Division.
On arriving in Flanders in early April after a hard time during Operation 'Michael', the 9th (Scottish) Division took over a sector of the front line south east of Ypres, straddling the Comines Canal. Only the part south of the canal was directly affected by 'Georgette'. Facing the devastated village of Hollebeke and with a scatter of woods behind it, the division described the forward area as a 'featureless and desolate waste of shell holes, where it is hard enough to locate one's position in broad daylight

and with the aid of a map, and all but impossible in darkness'. Large drafts arrived to take the place of those recently lost, and the division was still reorganising when the attack struck. Before we visit those units that faced the initial German assault, carried out by *7th Division*, it is illuminating to see events through the eyes of a battalion that had been relieved for rest on 9 April: the 7/Seaforth Highlanders, who did not complete their move to Seddon Camp near Vierstraat until 2.30am on 10 April.

> '1pm, 10 April. News came through that [the] Bosche had attacked and had made progress south of, and in the neighbourhood of, Wytschaete, and the old danger of a swinging flank looked like being realised again.
>
> Orders and counter-orders followed in rapid succession. First, to reconnoitre an old line of trenches running parallel to the Vierstraat – Parret Farm road [presumably to act as a reserve line] … The commanding officer and others had just allotted the first platoon area on this line when a mounted orderly arrived, steaming, with a led horse for the CO to ride hot foot to brigade for fresh orders.
>
> 2pm. These second orders cancelled the defensive line mentioned, and substituted orders to get ready to take up a line across the south-east aspect of Wytschaete – presumably to fill a gap left by somebody or other.
>
> 3.30pm. The third set of orders arrived just as the CO had just finished explaining the previous ones to the company commanders. The battalion was now detailed to take up a line from the Stables (White Chateau), where contact would be made with the Royal Scots, to Goudezeune Farm. This had been territory held by 19 Division, but whether it was held by anyone now was not clear.
>
> The men had tea while they stood to arms and the battalion marched off to take up its new line at 4.30pm … On its way to the [Dammstrasse] the battalion had to pass through an enemy barrage which killed several men and wounded others.'

The Seaforths were advancing into a complex, confused and rapidly-changing situation. At about 1pm, German infantry had attacked the outpost line being held by 26 (Highland) and 27 (Lowland) Brigades and forced the battalions that had been holding them to withdraw. The main line of defence facing Hollebeke, known as Oak Support, was still held, manned by A Company of 11/Royal Scots. This battalion had been

Weißes Schloß

The remnants of 'White Chateau', home of the wealthy industrialist Mahieu family, stood at the northern end of the 9th (Scottish) Division's line.

holding the entire front of 27 Brigade and had even been tasked with extending its line by 500m the previous night, taking over ground from the 9/Welsh of 19th Division. Two of its companies were north of the canal, so it was only half a battalion - holding a line that would usually be held by two or three – that was struck in the initial German assault. It was little short of a miracle that A Company managed to keep its hold on Oak Support. Two distinct attacks were beaten off, and the battalion's D Company came forward from a support position at the White Chateau to join it and create a defensive flank on the right. Eventually, 7/Seaforths arrived at the Dammstrasse and proceeded to push out patrols up the rising ground towards Ravine Wood, and through Pheasant Wood to Denys Wood. They came across an isolated detachment of the 9/Welsh and a 'few oddments' of the 6/Wiltshires – and, to their surprise, two companies of the 8/Black Watch, who were found digging in at the wrong place. This battalion of 26 Brigade, which had also been in a short period of rest at Vierstraat, had been ordered at 3pm to move to reconnoitre the area east of Grand Bois and discover the situation on the right of 27 Brigade. The Seaforths reported that 'not without difficulty these people were sorted out' and by 6.20pm brigade understood that the line was now held from the Stables, to Delbske Farm, then through Ravine Wood to the southern edge of Denys Wood and on to Goudezeune Farm. South of there it was believed that 58th Brigade of the 19th Division had been holding from Pick House to Torreken Farm, but that left a very wide and most concerning gap across the area of Oosttaverne Wood: this was, as we have seen, where the 6/Wiltshires and 9/Welsh Fusiliers had been nigh-on destroyed. Tensions increased when, at 8pm, 26 Brigade reported its belief that the 19th Division had evacuated Wytschaete altogether. It was later confirmed that all the area behind the 9th Division's new line was clear of enemy troops. There was more cheering information at 8.20pm, when it was learned that the South Africans were on the Messines road at Four Huns Farm.

During the day, 62 Brigade of the 21st Division had been placed at the disposal of 26 Brigade, and during the night it was ordered to secure Wytschaete and to reach before dawn a line between Pick House and the southern end of Onraet Wood. Employing 2/Lincolnshire Regiment on its left and 12/13th Northumberland Fusiliers on the right, the brigade achieved its objectives by 5am on 11 April. It was a considerable feat: a very dark night, little time to organise, and an advance across destroyed ground, with few present who knew the area at all. The contemporary reports provide a rather mixed picture of the resistance that was faced: the Lincolns reported meeting only a few enemy patrols, taking fourteen prisoners of *Magdeburgisches Pionier-Bataillon 4* and *Thüringisches Infanterie-Regiment 393* (both of *7th Division*), and *Reserve-Infanterie-Regiment 76* (*17th Reserve-Division*), 'and [we] killed a good lot more by Lewis gun and rifle fire'. The Northumberland Fusiliers reported eighty casualties after encountering German infantry and machine gun detachments moving forward through Wytschaete; hand to hand fighting ensued for half an hour and German artillery fired a barrage before the Fusiliers overcame resistance and pressed on.

At 5.30am a second advance began, driving the position a few hundred metres to a 'Corps Line' between Torreken Farm and Somer Farm.

During the rest of the day, heavy artillery bombardments and several infantry attacks fell on the division, but all were beaten off and no significant change to the position took place. It was however necessary, as the 19th Division fell back from Messines, for two companies of the 7/West Yorkshire Regiment to come forward from reserve to form a flank defence stretching back to Bogaert Farm. Brigade would later report that 'under very heavy shelling the battalion moved forward splendidly and their steadiness undoubtedly saved the situation'. Wytschaete remained in British hands until 16 April.

The road from Staenyzer crossroads into Wytschaete, in happier days. Like Messines, the village had been reduced to ruins in 1917.

The very busy day that the 7/Seaforths had on 11 April should not be neglected. It began in the night with a surprise arrival: a complete company of the 9/Welsh Fusiliers, intact after sheltering all the previous day in a dug-out at Denys Wood and still in telephone contact with their brigade headquarters until ordered to evacuate during the evening. This welcome addition was absorbed into the Seaforths' line on the Dammstrasse. This helped the battalion to send its own D Company, along with half of the pioneers, the 9/Seaforths, to fill the apparent gap down towards Wytschaete, where it was believed there were some of the 8/Black Watch. Things were still in a state of flux when the first German attack began, at about 8am. 'Both the weather and the situation were a bit hazy', according to the 7/Seaforths' diarist; and when large numbers of men began to approach Ravine Wood it was by no means immediately clear whether they were enemy or friendly troops. In this instance, uncertainty proved a good thing, for fire was held until the figures were only 150 yards distant and they took a great toll. 'The remainder of the Bosche lay down under cover of a patch of wood, to reconsider the matter.' Two patrols went out under Sergeant Jeffries and Corporal Mackay, intending a pincer movement against the prone enemy; on spotting the danger and rising to escape, the Germans were shot down. Jeffries clubbed one man with the butt of his rifle. The diarist – evidently a witty fellow - reported that at this point, 'those of the enemy surviving put up a white flag and sank on their knees in supplication'.

A hastily-arranged composite 'Kemmel Hill Defence Force' came into existence during the day, consisting of units of the 49th (West Riding) Division. They included the divisional pioneers, 19/Lancashire Fusiliers; 456th (West Riding) Field Company RE, attached to which was a platoon from each of the 5/, 6/ and 7/West Yorkshire; D Company of 49th Machine Gun Battalion; and 146th Trench Mortar Battery. Placed under the command of a Boer War veteran, Lieutenant Colonel Hugh Bousfield of the Leeds Rifles (West Yorkshire Regiment), it was positioned on the lower slopes of the hill.

The second day on Messines Ridge, 11 April.
While the 7/Seaforths were carrying out their blood-curdling counter-attack up on the Dammstrasse, the Germans finally wrested Messines and the crest of the ridge from British grasp. It was a significant and encouraging moment, for their view now opened up to the not too-distant objective of the Flemish Hills and, beyond them, the supply lines to Ypres.

108 Brigade of the 36th (Ulster) Division had also been sent from the Somme to Flanders to recuperate after severe fighting in Operation Michael. Its hopes for a quieter time were soon dashed, for it found itself under shell fire when it arrived by train at Poperinge on 9 April and five men were wounded right away. Early next day, it was ordered to the Kemmel defences and was placed at the disposal of the 19th Division. At 12.20am on 11 April, the brigade was ordered to come under the command of 57 Brigade and to move forward to reinforce the British units clinging on to the western edge of Messines. The three battalions were in place by 7am and all remained relatively quiet during the morning.

At 1pm, by which time enemy shellfire had become heavy, 108 Brigade heard that German forces were advancing northwards from the Ploegsteert area after their continued attack against the 25th Division. This represented a very considerable threat to the units holding on at Messines and Wytschaete. It was decided to throw out a defensive flank along the Messines-Wulverghem road and a warning order was given by division at 2.15pm, saying that if Hill 63 should fall to the enemy they would have to give up all ground and pull back to a line running just east of Wulverghem.

Before any further news came of enemy progress at Hill 63, the Germans renewed their attack against Messines, notably in the area between Pick House and Four Huns Farm, which was being held by the terribly depleted South African Brigade, now reinforced by the 1/Royal Irish Fusiliers of 108 Brigade. The latter included 125 men of a draft that

61

The height of Hill 63, seen here from the northern approach, down the main road from Messines. (Author)

had only arrived the previous day. Exactly what happened is difficult to report: some sources talk of an initial loss and then a successful counter-attack by the South Africans and Irish, a result of which was a congratulatory telegram from the 19th Division, but it is not even mentioned in the war diary of the latter or of 58 Brigade or the division. A second attack began at 7pm: the 1/Royal Irish Fusiliers, soon reinforced by two companies of 12/Royal Irish Fusiliers, reported that they were holding on but units on their left were giving way.

Records now show that twenty-four officers and men of 1/Royal Irish Fusiliers lost their lives on this day. With one exception, none of them have a known grave today and they are commemorated many miles from where they died, on the Tyne Cot Memorial. He is hardly representative of all, but the background of one soldier is illustrative of the mix of men that now made up what had originally been battalions of professional soldiers. Private 41675 Cassio Sherlock was born in Brazil in 1883 to a British father and Brazilian mother. In late 1915, then working as a clerk in Liverpool, he attested during the short-lived existence of the Derby Scheme (a group system of recruiting) and was called up to join the Army Service Corps in March 1916. A year later, he went to France. On 1 January 1918 he was compulsorily transferred to the infantry and posted into the battalion. Despite his inexperience as a front-line soldier, Sherlock had survived Operation 'Michael' but lost his life somewhere on the road north of Messines. Several others who died that day had regimental numbers very near to Cassio, which suggests that the battalion had quite a number of these transferred men of the Army Service Corps.

Hill 63 did fall to the enemy when it renewed its attack against 7 Brigade at about 6pm. By 8.40pm, the reserve battalion of 108 Brigade, 9/Royal Irish Fusiliers, which was located south of the Wulverghem road, was reporting that it was now coming under German machine gun fire. The game was up so far as hopes of holding onto Messines were concerned. Orders were given to withdraw from 1am on 12 April, with outposts remaining in place until 2am, and all units were to be on the Wulverghem Line by 4am. The new line would run from Bogaert Farm to In de Kruisstraat Cabaret, round the east of Wulverghem and then curving back to make a south-facing flank south of the village.

Nieppe and the Railway.

The parallel and straight pair of railway and road leading from Armentières to Bailleul became a key axis of the battlefield over the period 10 to 13 April. Successive British retirements took place along this axis as major German breakthroughs exposed it on both flanks. To the west, German forces exploited their early crossing of the Lys at Bac St Maur to capture Steenwerck by the end of 10 April. Within twenty-four more hours, the eastern flank was also penetrated by the breaking of the 25th Division's line at Ploegsteert and Romarin. As previously noted, this situation forced the 34th Division to evacuate Armentières before it was enveloped from both flanks. The retirements were undertaken in the face of almost constant attack and shell fire, and took the fighting towards Bailleul, successively through Pont de Nieppe, Nieppe, Pont d'Achelles, De Seule and La Crèche.

Late on 10 April, 101 Brigade of the 34th Division was ordered to leave the line it had established on the north bank of the Lys facing Erquinghem-Lys, and to hold the railway as far north as Trois Arbres. Its orders were to prevent any further enemy movement in a north easterly direction. Although the battalions of the brigade came under intense machine gun fire from the direction of Ferme Hollebecque as they did so, they were in place by 5.30am next day.

The position was held throughout 11 April until at 4.30pm an officer arrived with divisional orders: they must retire again, this time to the area of La Crèche and nearby Pont de Pierre. The battalions were to follow the railway as far as Steenwerck Station (which, despite the name, was 1500m from the town) and then to strike off to the west to take up the position designated. The orders proved to be impossible to follow. It was evident that the retirement had either been observed in preparation, or a

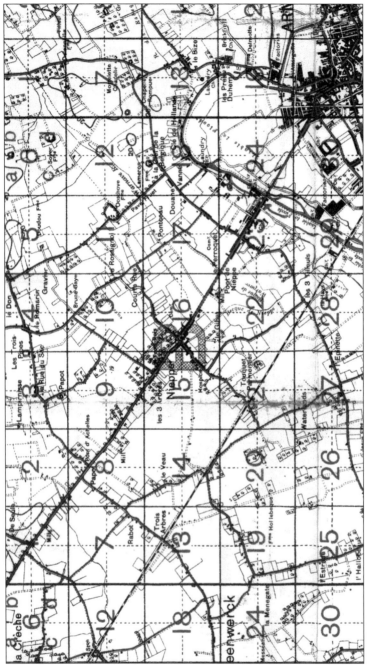

The British forces were gradually forced to withdraw along the road and railway towards Bailleul.

hostile attack was timed to commence at the same moment, for the roads, tracks and the whole area generally, suddenly came under sustained and heavy shelling which caused many casualties. The brigade's battalions (15 and 16/Royal Scots and 11/Suffolk Regiment, with some companies of 18/Northumberland Fusiliers attached) could only reach the appointed locations by circuitous routes, and although good order was in general maintained it was almost inevitable that there would be incidents where units lost their way and connection between them was broken. To make matters worse, on arrival they found 74 Brigade already there (having been withdrawn from its earlier fight at Croix du Bac): the staff work that was supposed to manage such things had also broken down. There was nothing for it but to bivouac for the night, in effect in reserve, while 74 Brigade held the front line. No-one knew of the presence of any British forces on the right (that is, west): in fact, help was in the process of arriving but little hard information about this was yet in the hands of 101 Brigade. The 29th and 31st divisions' lines had been broken and German forces were now streaming past the east side of Doulieu towards the higher ground in the Strazeele-Méteren area, but the 33rd Division was now deploying to hold this ground, with the 1st Australian Division not far behind them.

During 11 April, while 101 Brigade was still holding the line of the railway south of Trois Arbres, 88 Brigade held it from there up to Steenwerck Station. This formation, normally part of the 29th Division, had arrived in the area the day before 'amid a scene of utter confusion, the road being full of retiring troops and refugees' and 'strewn with the jetsam of war wagons, guns and wounded'. It had deployed from the railway across to the road at Papot and De Seule and was now stretched over a five kilometre front, much longer than even a brigade at full strength would normally be expected to hold, and was ordered to hold it at all costs. On the brigade's right front, 4/Worcesters and 2/Hampshires held the area between the road and railway, defending La Crèche. The 2/Monmouthshires and Royal Newfoundland Regiment were echeloned on the left flank. Patrols were pushed out to make contact with the 34th Division's units along the railway. The poor Newfoundlanders were at one point ordered to dump their packs and rush to a particular spot, but on getting there found a counter-attack had taken place and they were not needed. They never saw their packs again.

During the night, those elements of the 34th Division which had still been holding the outpost line beyond Nieppe were ordered to withdraw through the town and to pass through 88 Brigade behind them. They had begun to come under attack during the morning of 11 April, when the enemy forced a lodgement in the line near Burnley Post at Pont de

65

German troops of *Fourth Army* take a break in Nieppe before pressing on towards Bailleul. (Brett Butterworth)

Nieppe. It was found that troops supposed to retire on the immediate left of the brigade were not able to get into the position designated for them, causing the poor Monmouths to have to adjust again and dig in for the fourth time in twenty-four hours.

It seems extraordinary that the Germans did not appreciate that Nieppe had been evacuated until daylight on 12 April, for a formal attack with high explosive and gas shells was launched on the empty town. As 34th Division's diary notes, 'this is the more remarkable as during the night an enterprising enemy patrol had penetrated between the main and rear guard north of Nieppe'. It does, however, go on to say that the patrol was destroyed and its machine gun captured by 147 Brigade, so perhaps it is not so remarkable after all.

A small detail of information gained from a captured man of the German *Infanterie-Regiment 370* (*10th Ersatz Division*) may have raised eyebrows within British intelligence, for he said that Austrian artillery had been in action behind his unit. Although documentary evidence has not been found to confirm this, it is quite possible. At least twenty-two Austrian batteries had been moved to France to support Operation 'Michael', but most appear to have soon been withdrawn. There are references to Austrian guns taking part in 'Georgette'. This may also explain the burial in the military cemetery at Erquinghem-Lys of a man of an Austrian engineering or construction company.

During 12 April, 88 Brigade, which had been tasked with adjusting its line during the night but could only partially do so due to the mix-up between 74 and 101 Brigades, came under increasingly heavy attack from the newly arrived and fresh German *38th Division*. It held on and became a rallying point, on either side of which the defence of this area pivoted. That it did so is at least in part due to it being supported by 121 Brigade of the Royal Field Artillery, which came under its orders from late on 10 April.

At 4pm an infantry assault was delivered on the left, in which 88 Brigade's 'foremost troops were swept away'; but the German advance was temporarily held by two companies of the Newfoundlanders, who then withdrew a short way to the crossroads at De Seule. Across the road, two other companies of the battalion carried out what was described by brigade as a brilliantly executed counter-attack that pushed the enemy away, allowing 23/Northumberland Fusiliers to come forward from reserve and dig in. Sadly, the Newfoundlander's own records are rather fragmented and appear to have been written well after the day, leaving the detail somewhat fuzzy: what cannot be disputed is that the regiment lost six officers and 170 men in this affair. Of the fifty-nine who died on 12 or 13 April, just three have graves within the area of battle. The majority have no known resting place and are commemorated on the memorial at the Newfoundland Memorial Park at Beaumont-Hamel on the Somme.

Nieppe had been a rear area town since 1914 but suffered severe damage as the Germans advanced through it in the Battle of the Lys. (Author)

By the evening, the brigade's situation had become precarious: the right, near the railway, was holding well, although unnerved by news that the enemy had also broken past 74 Brigade; the left was being outflanked by large German forces advancing towards Neuve Église. Next day, the attacks in that area intensified. The 88 Brigade held on in its uncomfortably exposed salient for much of the day but, with a gap of about 1500m to any other British troops on the left, at 8pm it was inevitably ordered to retire towards Mont de Lille, in front of Bailleul.

On 13 April, 101 Brigade, still west of the railway, learned of the large scale attacks being launched across to the east at Neuve Église, and at 3.30pm that day came under attack themselves from the direction of Outtersteene. As with so many of these actions, weight of numbers eventually made the difference, and the brigade withdrew to a new line facing south west, in front of the railway at Bailleul.

German casualties mounted as the British organised reserves and an increasingly stubborn defence. (Brett Butterworth)

Chapter Five

The Fight for Neuve Église

By the end of 12 April 1918, further German progress against the 25th and 19th Divisions had brought the front close to Neuve Église. Within another forty-eight hours this tactically very important village had been lost to a further German attack, but only after desperate and intensive efforts to hold it had been overcome.

In 1914 a relatively small place, centred around its over-sized church, Neuve Église has a very long history of settlement and in medieval times had a population of some 10,000, making it a large and important town of textile workers. It sits on one of a chain of peaks of an undulating ridge, which, even though they are only seventy to eighty metres in height, are dominant. This ridge, which also incorporates the summits at Hill 63 near Ploegsteert, Crucifix Corner, Ravelsberg and Mont de Lille (all of which lie between Neuve Église and Bailleul), branches off westwards from the north-south orientated Messines Ridge as it dips into the Douve valley. By 1918 the village was surrounded by camps of huts, used for the shelter of troops moving into or out of the line. Much of the fighting, especially to the south and west of the village, took place amongst these camps.

GHQ's decisions to send reserves to the battle area were finally beginning to take effect and to give some hope to the beleaguered 25th and 19th Divisions. As part of the move of the 33rd Division from the south, the units of its 100 Brigade arrived at Caestre on 11 April. After marching via Méteren and observing crowds of refugees and much military traffic heading away, the brigade arrived at Ravelsberg Camp, west of Neuve Église. The current situation was ascertained from the headquarters of the 25th Division, and orders were received for the brigade's 2/Worcestershire Regiment to relieve the 4/KOYLI east of Neuve Église and for the rest of the brigade to extend the line southwards down to Romarin. There they would make contact with 75 Brigade, which was in the process of retiring to that place. The line to which they had been ordered was a pre-prepared position with barbed wire defences, often referred to in the war diaries as the 'Army Line'. Brigade ordered the 16/King's Royal Rifle Corps (KRRC), a battalion originally formed by members of the Church Lads' Brigade, to fill the line between the Worcesters and Romarin, while its 9/Highland Light Infantry (the

NEUVE-ÉGLISE   Coin du Marché et Rue d'Ypres

Edit, Verbrugge

The church and market square at Neuve Église witnessed considerable slaughter during the British counter-attack on 13 April 1918. (Author)

Glasgow Highlanders) would remain in reserve. The KRRC never did quite reach Romarin, as by the time they were arriving it was already in German hands. During the evening, B Company of 33rd Machine Gun Battalion arrived to reinforce the brigade.

On the arrival of the Worcesters, 4/KOYLI shifted leftwards but remained to prolong the line on the Worcesters' flank. The new arrivals' position lay astride the road from La Trompe Cabaret down to Petit-Pont, just outside Neuve Église and with an excellent field of fire and observation as far as Messines Ridge. Conversely, it could also be seen by the enemy. There was a gap between them and the 16/KRRC, which came into position on Leinster Road, south of the village, and stretched down towards Romarin.

12 April
At dawn the Worcesters sent out two patrols, under Second Lieutenants Harry Nicklin and Albert Parry, which very soon encountered large numbers of enemy. The patrols carried out their orders to hold any intended advance at bay for several hours, and it was only after being spotted from the air that they came under heavy shellfire and became increasingly in danger of being surrounded. Prudently, they then withdrew to rejoin their battalion's line. During this time, masses of German troops could be observed in the distance, apparently moving

from Messines towards Ploegsteert and, more worryingly, field and machine guns came up and engaged the Worcesters from very close range. Nicklin was awarded the Military Cross for his work, but was killed in action on 16 April. A former ranker, he was a member of the Evesham Rowing Club and a former chorister at St. Peter's Church at nearby Bengeworth. It is not known whether he ever received the news that his brother William, a corporal in the Royal Field Artillery, was killed on 13 April.

The day remained relatively quiet until about 4pm, when the KKRC noticed that British troops on their right were falling back, and took steps to use two platoons of their support company to create a south-facing defensive flank. The retirement was that of what remained of the 2/South Lancashire, 6/South Wales Borderers and 8/Border. At 6.15pm, a company of the Glasgow Highlanders moved to Kortepyp Cabaret. They soon detected that the enemy had advanced and almost reached the Neuve Église – De Seule road, and there was a serious gap on the right of the KKRC. This was a concerning development, for it meant the possibility of a German encircling movement being able to advance up the slope towards Neuve Église from the south. The 'minimum reserves' of the Worcesters and KRRC, which had been 'left out of battle' for such a purpose, were ordered to move towards the gap. During the night, the Glasgow Highlanders, moving its two reserve companies into the area between Aux Trois Rois Cabaret and Neuve Église, used its others to dig in astride the Kortepyp road. At the same time, 88 Brigade, which was on the far, southern, side of the gap sent its Newfoundland Regiment into the area, but at no time was the gap fully closed, leaving the right of the KRRC exposed.

At about 7.30pm a German attack against the KOYLI also threatened the Worcesters, but it was beaten off. News also came that the KRRC was under attack and, in order to counter any movement from that direction, the Worcesters' C Company was ordered to form a defensive flank position in Neuve Église itself. This was around the junction where the Kortepyp and Ravelsberg roads meet, forming a crossroads with the Dranoutre and Ypres roads. The battalion's headquarters was now moved from a concrete dugout on the Petit-Pont road into the more central and less exposed position of the brewery, near the church in Neuve Église.

During the night, the 4/York & Lancaster Regiment of 148 Brigade (also known as the Hallamshire Battalion) arrived in the area and took up a position to the north east of Neuve Église. They had endured a frustrating two days of successive retirements under shell fire from the area of Grande Munque Farm after being ordered there on 11 April, as units to their left and right either gave way under attack or were ordered to withdraw without informing the battalion. The Hallamshires now formed a line with the remnants of 8/Gloucesters on their left and 4/King's Shropshire Light Infantry (KSLI) and 4/KOYLI to their right, the latter linking up with the Worcesters.

13 April
Early in the misty morning of 13 April, another German attack broke through and around the 16/KRRC's position. The battalion suffered heavy casualties: the description in its war diary bears no resemblance to reports made by other units (it appears to have been written by an officer who was left with the reserve) and makes no mention of coming under attack, although it later lists eight officers who were killed, wounded or missing on 13 April. No fewer than fifty-six officers and men of the battalion are known to have lost their lives on this day, of whom just two have a known grave. Among the men said to be wounded and missing was the attached American Medical Officer, First Lieutenant William Staggers, who was taken prisoner.

In the German sweep forward, two of the three sections of 33 Machine Gun Battalion that had been deployed to support the infantry were hotly engaged but ultimately suffered very badly, losing all but two guns and their teams. Number 1 Section and the only remaining two guns of Number 3 moved to join the 2/Worcesters.

Little wonder that the British were under great pressure, for they were under attack by two German corps: on the British right, mainly facing the 34th Division, was *II Bavarian Corps*, employing a total of six divisions. On their left, aiming directly at Neuve Église, came *X Reserve Corps*, with two divisions. The German attack had some considerable difficulties, not least in coordination between the two corps, which led to a good deal of rancorous discussion later in the day. A significant problem had occurred when the line of advance of the right-hand of *II Bavarian Corps*, *117 Division*, came under fire from the artillery of the left hand of *X Reserve Corps*, *214 Division*. It was the latter division which was advancing into the 16/KRRC and, despite their success against that battalion, the division suffered serious losses on this day and was ultimately relieved by *11 Bavarian Division*.

Fast-moving German infantry now penetrated into Neuve Église along Leinster Road: they paid dearly for their enterprise, for a counter-attack by the Worcesters' C Company and a detachment under Second Lieutenant Arnold Pointon near the church is said to have killed sixty men and taken twenty more as prisoners. The Hallamshires also sent up a party of fifty men under Captain John Wortley and Lieutenant William Gifford: the battalion's war diary notes that they took fifty-one prisoners

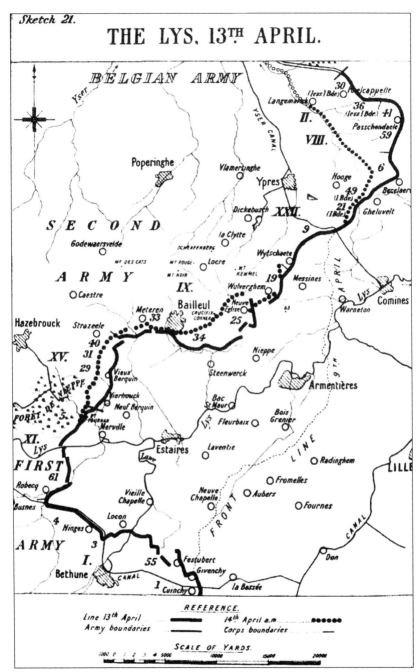

A map from the British Official History, showing the Allied front line and German gains on 13 April 1918.

before they ended at a location south and south west of the village, 'with oddments of battalions of 100th Brigade near them'. Wortley was killed later in the day, at about 8pm, when he was leading and encouraging a group of about forty stragglers from the KRRC back into a front line position. The 4/KOYLI sent their headquarters and support company, and they reported taking seventeen prisoners in what had been a YMCA canteen. It came at a considerable cost to their own officers: two killed and three wounded. The war diary of 33 Machine Gun Battalion, not one to downplay its achievements, reported that the square around the church was 'piled with corpses'. The various reports all point to the fighting in the centre of the village being severe, bloody and at very close quarters.

By the middle of the day, the 'oddments' holding the Germans off from Neuve Église were the Worcesters' C Company, joined by two platoons of the 9/Highland Light Infantry within the village centre; three officers and forty men of the 16/KRRC astride Leinster Road, with the rest of the Worcesters on their right. Together they made a more or less continuous line of defence running around the south side of the village; but great anxiety remained regarding what appeared to be a gap to the west and enemy pressure on the line was continuous.

By 2pm the situation was becoming concerning for the Hallamshires, still dug in around La Trompe Cabaret, for it was all too obvious that the

The position of the 2nd Worcesters in Neuve Église at midday on 13 April 1918.

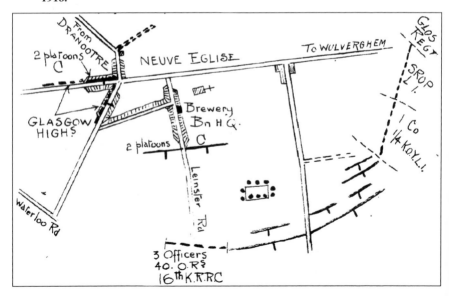

This view of Neuve Église, which appears to have been taken from the original town hall, shows on the left the large hospice building that was defended so stoutly by the Worcesters. Beyond it is Stampkotmolen Windmill. (Author)

Germans were in Neuve Église and likely to surround the battalion from its right-rear. The 4/KOYLI were also under pressure and carried out a local counter-attack at about 5pm.

At 6.30pm, the Worcesters' headquarters was moved into a building described in many histories as the Mairie (town hall) but which was in fact a former hospice, situated north of the crossroads, on the Dranoutre road. The Mairie, which in this Flemish-speaking area would more properly be referred to as the *Gemeentehuis*, faced the church in the village centre and may have been abandoned due to damage. A new and rather grander town hall was rebuilt there after the war. The hospice building gave the battalion a good view down a slope towards the village centre, but it was somewhat overlooked from higher ground on its western side. The building was to be manned as a strongpoint: two platoons would go into its cellars and be ready as a last reserve; the headquarters details and one platoon would provide defence of the building; another platoon would occupy a house on the same side of the road, forty metres further down to the crossroads. They were issued with a large supply of hand grenades and would act as a buffer between any enemy advance and the garrison of the Mairie. Lewis gun teams and a Vickers team that had just arrived (under Corporal 70727 Peter McBride of 33rd Machine Gun Battalion) would man the ground floor windows, covering the open ground at the rear and also down towards the village centre, and three riflemen would be at each window. All was set for a siege, should need be, except that, due to continued enemy attacks on the companies holding the line, it proved impossible to find the two platoons for the cellars. Ominously, as the evening wore on, none of the runners sent out to determine what was happening to the front line companies ever returned. To add to the dilemma, in making the move to the Mairie, telephone communications with brigade appear to have been lost.

A German push in between the Glasgow Highlanders at Aux Trois Rois Cabaret and the left of the Worcesters pierced the link between the two. It set the scene for an epic last stand action that lasted for the next twenty-four hours. As soon as it was dark, a series of flares were seen being fired in the village, soon followed by a small party of German soldiers making their way towards the rear of the Mairie. The Vickers gun opened fire and dispersed them, but itself then came under heavy, concentrated fire, which knocked it out. The resourceful McBride then found another; he is also said to have shot the arms of Germans who were trying to throw grenades into the doors and windows and brought his gun into action on numerous occasions during this fighting. The citation of his well-earned Distinguished Conduct Medal noted his 'supreme contempt of danger'. More flares went up around the crossroads and German machine gun fire poured onto the building from that direction and from the higher ground. Rifle grenades silenced a machine gun at the crossroads, but heavy fire from the church (it was believed that a machine gun was on its roof or in the tower) continued. Without information front the front-line companies – no word came from them after 6pm - it was very difficult to understand the situation, but it increasingly appeared that the enemy had got around the position and was now pressing in full force through the village.

During the night, the general order from Second Army was for a withdrawal to a line from Bailleul Station, to Mont de Lille, then Waterloo Road and Neuve Église, with outposts in advance of that line: this was perhaps more in hope than expectation, for it was far from clear exactly which British units could do this.

14 April
By the morning of 14 April, the Worcesters' platoon that had been holding the separate house had been forced to withdraw to the cover of the Mairie. Enemy movement could now be observed in almost every building in the village and on the open ground in front of the church. Lewis gun and rifle fire was poured onto the area from the Mairie, which in turn now received attention from trench mortars. Two shells burst inside the building,

causing many casualties; machine gun fire came in from three directions and sniper fire was directed against the back door and windows: it was a perfect scene of hell, and by 8am it was apparent that the garrison of the Mairie was completely surrounded. Unless something could be done, it was all too evident that the whole garrison would die or be taken prisoner.

Some acts of personal bravery stand out because of official recognition; others have now been lost as the memories of the survivors have died with them. Second Lieutenant Anthony Johnson MC, who had the day before carried information between headquarters and the front line companies, stepped forward and volunteered to break out to take urgent information to brigade. He was never heard of again and the details of his fate are unknown although his regiment's history suggests that he 'made his way out of sight, but before he could pass through the German lines he was hit and mortally wounded'.

Acting Captain John Crowe and Second Lieutenant Arnold Pointon now stepped forward. Crowe, who had served in the regiment since 1897 and until the end of March had been its Regimental Sergeant Major, volunteered to lead out a small party of men with a view to clearing the enemy from the rear of the building. They at first attacked towards a group of sheds just north of the Mairie. They then attempted to reach the Dranoutre road, from where they could fire on enemy troops on the higher ground, but the party came under fire from the crossroads area. Leaving two NCOs and five men, who were soon joined by Pointon, to hold the road, Crowe took two others forward. Crawling along a roadside ditch until he could not be observed, Crowe took his men across the road and along a hedge line, which took them up onto the rise. There they opened fire and rushed the enemy. One of his men was killed in the attempt, but Crowe and his remaining comrade, assisted by the combined fire from Pointon's party and from the garrison in the Mairie, drove the Germans further away, killing several and capturing three machine guns. The immediate effect of Crowe's action was that the enemy could be seen retiring towards the crossroads, and his battalion's commanding officer, Lieutenant Colonel Gerald Stoney, seized the chance to send out runners to re-establish contact with British troops on his left and right. Nothing came from the latter, but contact was established on the left. At much the same time, at about 11am, an officer of a Corps School arrived saying that he had been sent into Neuve Église to assess the situation. Stoney sent him back with an urgent request for reinforcement by a battalion.

By 1pm it was becoming quite clear that the Germans were massing for a final attack to clear Neuve Église, and trench mortar and machine gun fire against the Mairie intensified. Crowe's party on the high ground

Another panoramic view of Neuve Église, this time from the church tower. The prominent hospice is easily spotted. (Author)

were still there, now very exposed. With no sign of the hoped-for reinforcement, Stoney ordered his men to evacuate. Reluctantly leaving three men who could not be removed, the garrison – which included at least twenty men who had been wounded – escaped without further loss, despite heavy machine gun fire being directed against them. In August 1918 John Crowe received the Victoria Cross from King George V. He is believed to be the only VC recipient already to have been wearing the ribbon of the Long Service and Good Conduct Medal. His comrade, Arnold Pointon, was awarded the Military Cross.

At about 5pm, by which time the *36th Reserve Division* had completely cleared Neuve Église, flares went up from Stampkotmolen Windmill on the high ground north of the village. They spelled trouble for the remnants of the Hallamshires, KOYLI and KSLI that had been holding on in the area of La Trompe Cabaret, for they were now in acute danger of being outflanked. There was nothing for it but to withdraw.

The withdrawal from the Ypres Salient.
At this point, with most of Messines Ridge, Ploegsteert and Neuve Église now in German hands, both sides begun to relieve the tired divisions that had taken the brunt of the fighting so far. For the Germans this meant bringing in fresh formations, ready to press the advance towards the original objectives. For the British, it meant taking a very hard and emotional decision.

By 12 April the *Sixth Army's* attack had brought it near to the high ground of the Strazeele ridge and Méteren. This exposed the key British-held town of Bailleul to attack from its south-west and western sides. As described in the *Objective Hazebrouck* volume that accompanies this book, the threat was blunted by the arrival of reserves: notably in the form of the 33rd and 1st Australian divisions, but also by the creation and deployment of an array of composite battalions made up from battlefield stragglers, army schools, cyclist units and anything that the high command could muster. Approval was even given to arm the Labour Companies. By 14 April, French divisions were beginning to arrive in the rear area. Further west, the 5th and 61st (South Midland) divisions had also arrived and held the enemy at the Forest of Nieppe. But there were no more reserve formations available. Second Army had already stripped its own reserves, but the *Fourth Army's* attack towards the Flemish Hills showed no real signs of slowing down. Field Marshal Sir Doulas Haig issued his famous 'backs to the wall' Special Order of the Day, but such a call to action was not enough. The only way to find more troops was to face up to the need to shorten the line at Ypres. Plans for such an eventuality had been drawn up as early as January 1918.

At 1pm on 14 April 1918, Major General Charles 'Tim' Harington (the Chief of Staff of the Second Army) issued Second Army Operation Order Number 19:

The hospice building was badly damaged during the siege. It was later rebuilt and now operates as a youth centre. (Author)

All attacks made yesterday have been successfully repulsed after severe fighting. Indications, however, point to the enemy bringing up fresh divisions to continue his attacks in the direction of Neuve Église and Méteren. In accordance with the instructions of the Field Marshal Commanding in Chief [Haig], the Army Commander [Plumer] has decided that the time has come when the Ypres Salient, which has been successfully held by this Army for so long, must be vacated. His decision is based solely on the necessity of economising troops.'

There was of course, another factor, not much voiced in the official paperwork: it was just possible that the German offensive would succeed and that the supply line to Ypres might be cut off. The fewer the men in the Salient, the less a defeat it would be.

Harington went on to outline the position to which the force should be withdrawn and gave an outline timetable over the period 14-16 April. He also said that:

'The essence of a successful withdrawal lies in deceiving the enemy. On no account is any destruction by fire or explosion to be carried out. ... There must be no movement whatever by day tomorrow which will indicate our withdrawal to the enemy.'

Withdrawal, of course, does not just mean a move for the infantry: the artillery, transport, dumps and stores, dressing stations, ordnance workshops and even the casualty clearing stations and railheads deep in the rear had to prepare to move. It was a major and risky undertaking, especially given the weight and speed of the attack that was underway not too far distant.

It would not be the first time that a British Army had voluntarily given ground at Ypres to the enemy in order to shorten the line: it had happened during the First and Second Battles in 1914 and 1915. But it was by far the most significant and reluctant, for it meant vacating the blood-soaked territory that had been won at such hideous cost in the Third Battle ('Passchendaele') in 1917. It also meant asking the Belgian Army, holding the line north of the British, to comply.

The withdrawal to the shorter line released three divisions: from 13 April, when it was being held (north to south) by the 30th, 36th, 41st, 59th, 6th, 49th and 21st Divisions (although some had already released individual brigades); the new line was now held only by the 36th, 41st, 6th and 21st.

Chapter Six

Bailleul Falls, 15 April 1918

The 59th (2nd North Midland) Division was holding the Passchendaele front when, on 10 April, it received word that the Salient was to be evacuated and the force pulled back to the Battle Zone. That same evening, its 178 Brigade was detached and sent to Dranoutre, where it came under the temporary orders of the 19th (Western) Division and would soon be engaged in fighting between Wulverghem and Kemmel. The battalions of the remaining 176 and 177 brigades were badly under-strength; 177 alone was some 900 men below its proper establishment. The reinforcement drafts that the division received they considered to be incapable 'of a sustained effort to stem the vigorous attacks of the enemy, elated with the extent of his advance'. The drafts, mostly of 18 year-olds, returned wounded and men combed out from the bases, would soon be put to the test.

The division had had an unusual war. Raised in 1914 as a second line Territorial Force reserve, it was hurried to Ireland in Easter 1916 to quell the nationalist rising and suffered considerable numbers of casualties there. It came to France in March 1917 and saw much action during the Third Ypres offensive, at Cambrai and in Operation 'Michael'. It had only arrived at Passchendaele on 5 April, still absorbing drafts and now very weak in junior leaders and men with battlefield experience. By the evening of 14 April the division had come out of the Ypres Salient and had concentrated at Locre.

During the night, it relieved the exhausted 34th Division and a bewildering array of scattered remnants of units of 74, 88 and 147 brigades in the area east of Bailleul. The Germans had been attacking this line during the day, and it was not expected that any great time would elapse before it all began again.

The south-facing line now occupied by the division was essentially along the undulating high ground that stretches from Neuve Église. To some extent, the fighting that followed was defined by the attempt to hold a series of small peaks: Crucifix Corner and the Ravelsberg along the road from Aux Trois Rois Cabaret, Hill 70, lying to the north near Haegedoorne, and Mont de Lille, nearest to, and south east of, Bailleul. The ground drops steeply down from the latter and from the Ravelsberg,

Memorial to the British 34th Division, located at the summit of Mont Noir. It is very similar to the divisional memorial at La Boisselle on the Somme. (Author)

and whoever is in possession of them enjoys excellent observation over the town, the Flemish Hills to the north and the Lys plain to the south.

The British had made Bailleul their home in October 1914 and it had become a centre of considerable importance for military purposes and for the rest and recreation of the troops. The line to which the British forces had fallen back, running across the southern outskirts, was of no great tactical value and there had already been discussions about abandoning the town, but there was a considerable emotional reluctance to do so. With its origins before Roman times, by 1914 Bailleul was a pleasant market town with a population of more than 13,000: the total destruction of the town in April 1918 inevitably led to its depopulation and this figure was not attained again until the 1960s. Bailleul had an impressive town hall and churches; several large schools and a lunatic asylum were used by Casualty Clearing Stations. A light railway network ran around Mont de Lille and past the Ravelsberg, by means of which the Wulverghem and Messines front had been supplied. Numerous camps of army huts dotted the area and three airfields had been established in fields on the east and north east sides of the town.

Several large buildings in Bailleul had long since been put to use by British casualty clearing stations, including this boys' school. (Author)

The division's 176 Brigade took up the right of the line, skirting the southern outskirts of Bailleul from the Steam Mill to Mont de Lille, placing all three of its battalions in line. As this left it with no reserve on which it could call, division allocated two companies of its pioneers, 6/7th Royal

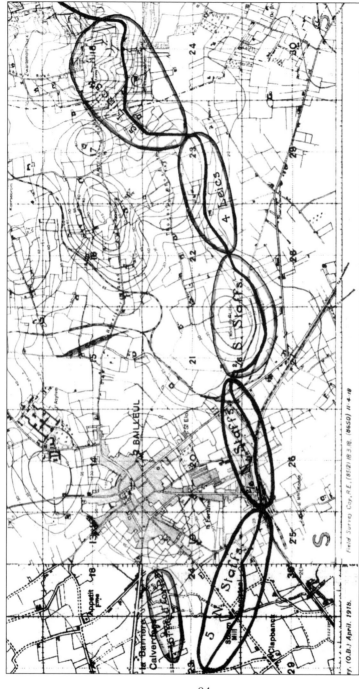

The battalions of the 59th (2nd North Midland) deployed onto the slopes of Ravelsberg Ridge.

Scots, to the brigade. On the left, 177 Brigade carried on the line from Mont de Lille to Crucifix Corner. It placed two battalions in the front line and kept one in reserve near Keersebrom. Beyond the divisional boundary came the 9/Norfolk Regiment and 1/Leicestershire Regiment of 71 Brigade (6th Division). Unfamiliar with the ground and attempting to relieve a variety of units, the brigades only finally got into position at about 6.30am on 15 April.

At midnight a local attack near the Steam Mill, west of Bailleul, caused the division's 467th Field Company RE to be deployed into the line on the extreme right, linking up with the left of the 33rd Division. There had been considerable localised fighting within the vicinity of the mill, which remained in German hands even after a determined counter-attack there by three companies of the 4 and 7/Duke of Wellington's on 14 April. Acting Captain Arnold Luty distinguished himself in this action, during which he was twice wounded. At his funeral in 1936, his old brigadier recalled, 'Luty dashed out at the head of his men, and drove the Germans out with the bayonet. He gained the Military Cross, and had he not been knocked out he would unquestionably have been a strong candidate for the VC.' Luty's brave act had at least not gone unnoticed: sadly the same cannot be said of many others that would take place over the next twenty-four hours, for the potential witnesses to such events were either dead, in enemy hands or moved down through the medical evacuation chain.

Within a very short time of completing the relief of the outgoing units, the battalions encountered hostile patrols probing forward. They were repelled, and 2/5th Lincolns of 177 Brigade (whose advanced posts were along Thornton Road, on the south side of Ravelsberg Ridge and stretching up to Mont de Lille), even managed to take fifteen Germans prisoner. But this good fortune could not last, as three German divisions were positioning themselves ready for an assault. One of them, a recently arrived and fresh formation named the *Alpenkorps* (Alpine Corps), although it was only a division in size, would play a key part in the fighting from this point until the end of the battle.

The German plan was not to attack Bailleul directly but to outflank it on both sides. On the left, *Sixth Army* would attack against Strazeele and Méteren: this is described in the *Objective Hazebrouck* companion to this book. *Fourth Army* would attack from just south of Wytschaete but focus on the high ground of Crucifix Corner, Ravelsberg and Mont de Lille. This would be attacked by *117 Infanterie-Division*, *11 Bavarian-Division* and *32 Infanterie-Division* with *11 Reserve-Division* in close support. The *Alpenkorps* would be positioned around the south of Bailleul and as far west as the Steam Mill. It amounted to one German division for each of the five British battalions holding this line.

From what appears to be noon onwards (the times given by each affected unit vary from 11am to 2pm), a bombardment of gas and high explosive began to fall on all of the division's line, causing heavy casualties. It also extended deep in the rear, to the railway and onto Bailleul itself. The two forward companies of the 2/6th North Staffs, positioned on the southern slope of Mont de Lille, suffered such damage that by the time the German infantry attacked later in the day only Second Lieutenant Swale and three men were left alive and unwounded. The story elsewhere was perhaps not quite as dramatic but was nonetheless similar in all units. C Company of 9/Norfolks, positioned in support near Crucifix Corner and detailed as counter-attack company, was so reduced in numbers that it could no longer carry out the task should the need arise: B Company stepped up from reserve. The 4/Lincolns, which was holding Crucifix Corner and the forward slope facing towards Westhof Farm and Neuve Église, also suffered badly.

The bombardment continued for two hours, at which point it became even heavier and is described as a barrage. From 2.45pm, local infantry

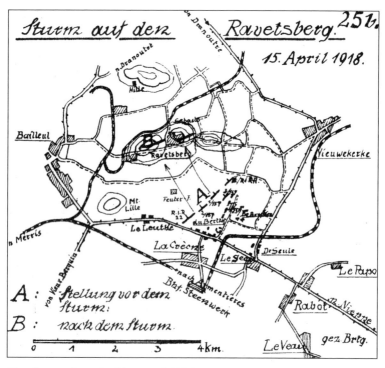

Sketch map from the history of *157th Infanterie-Regiment*, illustrating the attack on the Ravelsberg. (Jack Sheldon)

86

attacks against Crucifix Corner began: they were carried out by *Schlesisches Infanterie-Regiment 157* of *117th Infanterie-Division*, which advanced up the southern slope from the direction of De Broeken.

Successive assaults were repelled, and most units describe carrying out initially successful counter-attacks, but almost inevitably the line eventually gave way. Things were not helped by the British artillery presence being so weak (little more than 121 Brigade RFA) and short of ammunition. The 4/Lincolns said it was on their left that enemy troops broke through the position and reached the summit, despite the battalion having been reinforced by two companies of 2/4th Leicesters. They were forced to retreat northwards towards Keersebrom. The Germans could now dominate the battalion's position from above, and they quickly pushed westwards towards the next peak, the Ravelsberg. But the unit on the Lincolns' left, the 9/Norfolks, said that the problem was that it was the unit on their right that gave way. It is very difficult to know which is right, and German records that may have been the source of an answer no longer exist. In reality, it appears that the weight of the German attack broke through in multiple places at much the same time.

By 5.25pm, the 2/5th Lincolns, 2/6th North Staffords and 2/6th South Staffords were also deep in trouble and all were withdrawing towards the railway. They were only just ahead of large numbers of enemy troops, advancing down the slope from the Ravelsberg towards Bailleul and across the former aerodromes south of the asylum. The Lincolns reported that its left hand company, which had been in touch with the Leicesters on the Ravelsberg, fought to the last as it was engulfed, but in truth all of its companies suffered heavily. By the time it had been relieved later in the day, the 2/5th Lincolns had lost 352 men and four officers, of whom one was its commander, 42 year-old Boer War veteran Harold Roffey. He was one of the few men in the army to have been the recipient of the Royal Humane Society Medal, which was to recognise his bravery in rescuing three men from drowning in the Nant Fawr river at Cardiff in 1911. Roffey went to France in August 1914 as second in command of the 2/Lancashire Fusiliers, and was badly wounded in the jaw and mouth during the Battle of Le Cateau. Not content with a desk or training job, once he had made a recovery he badgered the authorities and was given command of the 2/5th Lincolns just before it left England for France. It is said that he died from wounds resulting from a shell burst, having ventured out of his battalion's line to reconnoitre during a quieter spell. His body was lost and apparently only found when British forces recaptured the area in September 1918. He was initially buried behind the railway cutting and exhumed from there for burial in Bailleul in 1919.

All of the British units which had been engaged in this fighting at the

Ravelsberg and Mont de Lille survived to fight another day, but all had lost very heavily. The three battalions of 176 Brigade reported a total of nineteen officers and 557 men dead, wounded or missing. Their withdrawal through to the west and north of Bailleul, or to Keersebrom and Hille, was completed before the day was out, during which they continued to come under artillery and machine gun fire while trying to reorganise and dig in on a new line. The fragmented and exhausted nature of the units in retirement, and the fact that there were no fresh units nearby who could join its defence, meant that there was little organised resistance to the German occupation of Bailleul around the town itself. 176 Brigade reported the German method of harassment of the withdrawal:

'Whilst engaged in reorganising on these lines, the men being formed up under cover of our patrols, strong enemy patrols which had been pushed out from Bailleul interrupted this work. Their method was to fire Very lights, machine guns and rifle fire, and then to rush forward in a 'V' formation, each patrol being about 20 men strong. They pushed through the gaps in our line which had not yet been filled, and caused a good deal of confusion to our men. Firing became general and it became impossible to distinguish friend from foe.'

It was also noted how much the Germans used flares and rockets to signal their position and to call upon artillery: 'On reaching Bailleul square two golden rockets were sent up and the enemy barrage at once lengthened to the north of the town'.

Hundreds of men made their way back, through or around Bailleul, and soon approached the area where the various scattered units that had been relieved on 14 April had settled. They were now digging in a reserve trench line and had stood to arms while the shells were raining down on the far side of Bailleul. Stragglers from the fighting at Mont de Lille came into 147 Brigade's area, where about 350 officers and men of 5/North Staffs were gathered together and put into the line under the orders of 4/Duke of Wellington's. The rest drifted through and were assembled around Locre in order to reorganise. Information given by the stragglers painted a bleak picture: the commanding officer of 2/6th North Staffs, Lieutenant Colonel James Porter, told the 11/Suffolks that his battalion 'and probably the whole brigade, was broken'. It was the truth.

The loss of Bailleul was a considerable blow and a matter of universal regret to the British, not least from the point of view of morale, and an encouragement to German ambitions to capture the Flemish Hills. By the end of 15 April the town, now battered, was securely in German hands.

New Zealand troops march through Bailleul in 1917. Although it was within range of aerial bombardment and the very longest range artillery, the town was largely intact before Operation 'Georgette'. (Author)

It would soon be turned into rubble by British artillery, firing to deny it to the Germans. Heavy artillery, for example, fired against a large observed build-up of enemy troops in the area of the airfields and asylum; later aerial reports described seeing hundreds of German dead. By 16 April the town was reported as being in a 'sea of flame'. Within a few days scarcely a single original brick of the town was still standing.

The 59th (2nd North Midland) Division had, effectively, been withdrawn (with the exception of 5/North Staffs, now north west of the town) and the detached 178 Brigade was some distance away, north of the Douve. The British front had been pushed back to the area between Bailleul and St. Jans Cappel, and the familiar names of the tired 147, 101, 74 and 103 brigades once again made up the right-to-left order of battle along the line.

On the right, Méteren was still in the hands of the 33rd Division, and across the Douve the line ran across the south of Kemmel to Wytschaete.

A human footnote can be added to the story of the fall of Bailleul. In

89

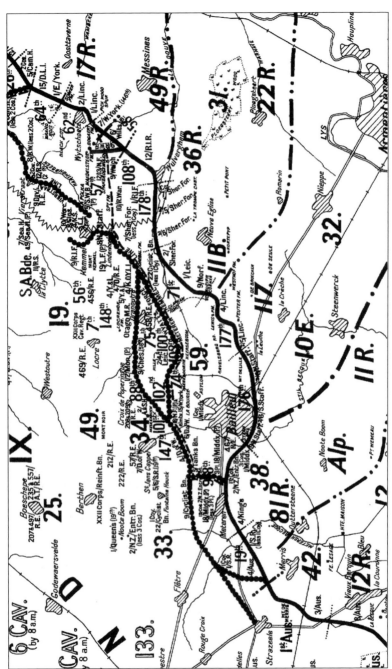

Part of a map from the British Official History, illustrating the Allied front line and German gains on 15 April 1918.

Once Bailleul fell into enemy hands, British artillery turned its attention on the town. By the end of the war there was virtually nothing left. (Author)

1936, British newspapers carried an appeal for information from a lad in Belgium who was unsure of his exact age and who had been given the name of Louis Delarue by the Sisters of Our Lady of Ypres. He had been abandoned, at an age estimated at eighteen months, on the Bailleul-Hazebrouck road when the town was being evacuated ahead of the German advance. The child was found by a British officer, who took him by lorry to St. Omer and then on to Rouen, where he was handed to the care of the Sisters. The officer is said to have visited the young Louis before the war ended, but after that all contact was lost. Whether poor Louis ever found further details of his family past, or of the officer who delivered him to safety, is unknown.

The old 59th (2/North Midland) Division did not survive its experiences in 'Michael' and 'Georgette'. Its losses and condition after the Bailleul fighting led to it being withdrawn in order to be completely rebuilt. In early May 1918 the infantry and pioneer battalions, brigade trench mortar batteries and machine gun battalion were reduced to training cadre establishment. All surplus men were sent to the base or drafted to other units. The division was then reconstituted, made up to strength with Garrison Guard battalions and was placed on rear defence construction duties. It was later reconstituted again and underwent training to enable it to hold a sector of the front line, eventually returning to action as a very different formation in late July.

Chapter Seven

Wytschaete Lost, 16 April 1918

We left the 9th (Scottish) Division holding on to Wytschaete and the Dammstrasse on 11 April, and the situation there was fundamentally the same four days later. The village lay just behind the right-hand of the division's front, which came up from the great mine crater of Spanbroekmolen and ran along the main road on Messines Ridge before curving away between Onraet and Oosttaverne Woods. The latter was in German hands. The front line then ran for a short distance along the road from Oosttaverne towards Ypres before turning off to follow the line of the Dammstrasse.

Wytschaete was prised from the grip of the division on 16 April. On this day the Germans carried out two operations for local tactical advantage: to the south; *Sixth Army* finally wrested Méteren from the 33rd Division, but could advance no more. It had suffered severe casualties in the operation, and within forty-eight hours *Sixth Army* effectively abandoned 'Georgette', citing its exhaustion. From this point onwards, the focus of the German effort swung towards *Fourth Army* and its attempt to seize the Flemish Hills. In retrospect, the Battle of the Lys was now lost, in that the original strategic intentions were unlikely to be fulfilled – Foch had been saying so for several days – but there was much more fighting to come, and the capture of Wytschaete was a necessary first step for the Germans.

While the Germans had been successfully pushing on to capture Neuve Église and Bailleul, leaving Wytschaete sticking out in a more pronounced salient, as many British troops as could be gathered had been put to work on digging and erecting barbed wire defences for two new defensive lines. At around 3,200m behind the front, the first of these was the Vierstraat Line. It lay a little way east of, and parallel to, the road that ran up from Kemmel and La Polka, through Vierstraat crossroads towards Ypres. Another, the Cheapside Line, lay another kilometre further west.

South of Spanbroekmolen, in the area of IX Corps, the front line was held by six tired and under-strength brigades that had been fighting since 9 April, now all under the operational control of the 34th Division. Their improvised position was a poor one of shallow trenches and little barbed wire. They were cheered, though, by the arrival of more field artillery, from the 38th (Welsh) and 36th (Ulster) Divisions and even the French

28th Division d'Infanterie: with good cause, for the guns played the vital part in breaking up several attacks that were attempted by *10th Ersatz-Division*, *117th Infanterie-Division* and *32nd Infanterie-Division* against the Corps' line on 16 April. At the cost of considerable numbers of casualties, the German attack achieved only small dents in the British line astride the St. Jans Cappel and Locre roads.

From Spanbroekmolen northwards, the nine kilometres long front held by the 9th (Scottish) Division, which now also incorporated 62 and 64 Brigades (of the 21st Division) and 146 Brigade (of the 49th), came under a pulverising gas and high explosive bombardment from 5am (some say 4.30am). All telephone communications were cut, from which we can deduce that the division now largely, if not totally, lost the use of the network of buried cable that had been so helpful in the earlier fighting. Battalion signallers would now face the prospect of laying out and fixing breaks in ground lines while under fire: either that, or messages would need to be taken by runner or signalled by visual means. Not that there was much to signal to, for the division's front was covered by very little artillery and there were few infantry reserves on which it could call.

A feature of the fighting on the Lys was the British army's ability to form improvised composite units, made up of officers and men from a mixture of units. That they often fought to great effect, often at the shortest of notice and in unfavourable circumstances, is testament to their methods. Field Service Regulations and their training and experience had given these men a common language and doctrine which more than overcame the temporary loss of their regimental *esprit de corps*. In fact this arrangement was something that was common to other armies – for example the Germans, who were usually on the defensive for much of the war on the Western Front, had developed this system to a fine art. These units sometimes also had the advantage of being larger in manpower than the depleted units that they reinforced. Two of them would play a part at Wytschaete: sadly, there is no war diary for 2 Battalion of the 39 Divisional Composite Brigade; but it is mentioned in many others (for ease, we shall refer to it as 2/39 Composite); 3 Battalion (3/39) does have a very brief diary. Their own 39th Division had been so badly damaged during Operation Michael that a decision had been taken to reduce it to a cadre that would be used for training incoming American units. On 10 April, urgent orders came for the division to form five composite battalions from the men that it had left. It led to 2/39 Composite being formed from men of the 13/Gloucesters and 13/Sussex, and 3/39 to be made up of troops from 16/Sherwood Foresters, 17/KRRC and 16/Rifle Brigade. Both units arrived at Ridge Wood on 13 April and were placed under the command of 62 Brigade.

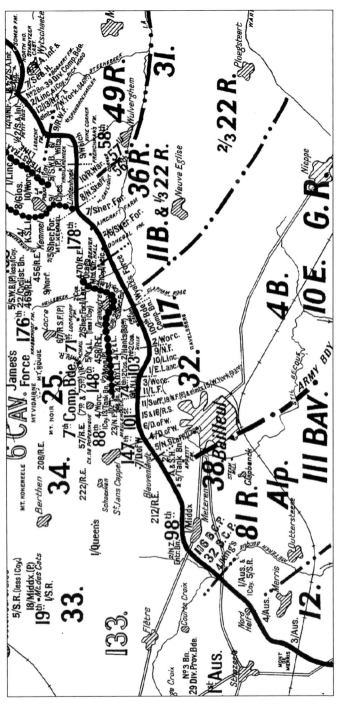

Part of a map from the British Official History, illustrating the extraordinary, fragmented nature of the British defences once Bailleul had fallen.

Once again greatly assisted by dense fog, the German infantry began to attack at 5.30am after an hour of intense shelling on the British front line, the village and all approaches. Within a very short time, Wytschaete fell. The breakthrough came in the area held by the 1/Lincolns. This battalion, the right-most of the two of 62 Brigade that were defending Wytschaete, had been holding from Staenyzer Cabaret to Scott Farm. It later said that the bombardment had remained on its front for another ten minutes after it had lifted elsewhere, and that the battalion had been under shellfire ever since coming into the line on the night of 12-13 April. With no shelter worth mentioning, casualties were heavy: two of the only twelve officers available, and eighty men. German infantry penetrated the battalion's position just north of Staenyzer Cabaret and then wheeled inwards. With the fog and smoke, visibility was so poor that it was impossible to get a clear idea of the situation: men in separated posts would have only seconds to identify figures as they loomed out of the fog or even to conclude that they were being attacked.

The battalion stood its ground until 7am, later reporting that not a man surrendered. Records of the Commonwealth War Graves Commission reveal that forty-six officers and men were killed in the attack, of whom only two have a known grave today. The rest, never recovered and identified, are listed on the distant Tyne Cot Memorial. The dead included experienced men that the battalion could ill-afford to lose (two were holders of the Distinguished Conduct Medal, including Company Sergeant Major 9362 Richard Lock) and committed soldiers like Private 16934 Reuben Copestake. He had previously served for seven years in the Militia and re-enlisted while working in New York City in December 1914.

That any men of the battalion got away to safety was due in part to an act of bravery by Acting Captain and now Adjutant of the 1/Lincolns, Frederick McKellar, a former ranker who had begun service as a drummer with the Gloucestershire Territorials. He was on the way up from battalion headquarters to assist in the defence when he encountered a party of the enemy. At once he went for them singlehanded, with revolver and bombs, firing at close quarters and checking their advance. McKellar's brave act enabled his commanding officer, Major Henry Wood Gush, to withdraw the final detachment of a handful of men that was hanging on at the Staenyzer Cabaret crossroads and to carry out a fighting retirement, including bringing back some wounded, through Wytschaete Wood to the next line of resistance. McKellar, who was awarded the Military Cross for his action (Gush got the Distinguished Service Order), was killed on 21 August 1918. He was aged 22.

Next in line to the Lincolns, the 7/West Yorkshires were holding the long line from Scott Farm to the Spanbroekmolen mine crater. Over half of its men were recently arrived drafts, many of them 18 year-olds. Records of their experience on 16 April 1918 are scanty indeed: the war diary has a single line 'enemy attacked'. They certainly did, and according to 62 Brigade the battalion was overwhelmed. The fact that the battalion lost forty-eight men dead, not one of whom has a known grave, stands as testament to a very difficult day. By 6.55am, a straggler from 1/Lincolns found his way to 156 Brigade RFA, which was headquartered at Parret Camp, near Vierstraat. He reported that the Germans had captured Spanbroekmolen. This meant that the way was open to Kemmel. But it was evident to the artillery that men were fighting on at Wytschaete. A man at its observation post at North House called to report that the infantry had been firing SOS rockets and that he could now see German infantry for himself. He was told to carry on and use his rifle: what happened to him we can only guess. Even by 8.05am, 62 Brigade headquarters was reporting by phone to the 9th Division that some 200 men were still fighting in the village: this seems highly optimistic and possibly based on badly out of date information.

The engulfing of these battalions suggests that the attacking force had an easy time. This, from German sources, was certainly not the case. There are reports that the assembly of the attacking force was badly disrupted by British artillery fire and that when the advance was made it met with such intense fire that it at first wavered. At 2pm, orders were given to cease the attack.

North of where the Germans were now streaming into the gap cut in the Lincolns' and West Yorks' position, the 12/13th Northumberland Fusiliers, reinforced by a company of 2/Lincolns, held its position despite coming under heavy attack and swung back to create a south-facing defence on its right flank. On the Fusiliers' left, D Company of 1/East Yorkshires lost an entire platoon killed or captured but otherwise also held on against an attack by the German *7 Infanterie-Division*. Together, these units eventually held from Somer Farm, through North House to Black Cot. Two companies of 8/Black Watch continued the position from there to the Vierstraat Line.

A co-ordinated and determined counter-attack to regain Wytschaete did not take place until 7.30am, but plans, orders and counter-orders concerning such an action had been passed about all day. The 2/Lincolns, which had been relieved the previous night and only arrived for rest at Rossignol Wood at 4am, received orders to stand to when the German shelling started just half an hour later. A counter-attack, employing the battalion and the 7/Seaforths, was contemplated and arrangements made during the morning, but was cancelled as the fog was now lifting. The ground over which such an attack would have to be made was completely open to observation from Wytschaete, Spanbroekmolen and the Peckham craters which were now also in enemy hands. 2/39 and 3/39 Composite Battalions, now at Ridge Wood, was also available for such an attack – and then came news from XXII Corps at noon that two French divisions were also coming into the area on the right of 62 Brigade and that they would attack to recapture Spanbroekmolen. This good news was very soon blunted, for French reinforcements were reduced to a single division (the 28th); then a plan to attack at 6.30pm was delayed for another hour because the French would not be ready. Before this final delay, the Lincolns, Composite Battalions and 7/Seaforths moved into their assembly positions. Or nearly so: the Seaforths found their allotted start line on the east side of Grand Bois so exposed to machine gun fire that they prudently decided to wait on the west side. Information came from a staff officer of the 9th Division who had been sent to liaise with the French: he could report no definite confirmation that the French were going to attack and, in the event, they did not. The small British force would be on its own – and it was told that its attack was conditional on its own artillery barrage actually starting on time. If that failed, the battalions would just have to dig in and shelter as best as they could.

The counter-attack did begin, at 7.30pm, just at the very moment that German shells began to fall on the "jump off" position: it had taken the Germans half a day to haul their field artillery forward, the result of a lack of horse transport and the devastated nature of the terrain. The 7/Seaforths, having to negotiate an initial move to get to their starting point on time, barely made it in the failing light. Only the head of the single file had reached the starting point when the British bombardment opened up, but the battalion found the British shelling to be too far ahead for it to provide effective cover anyway. Within five minutes, the Seaforths' pace picked up as German shells began to fall on Grand Bois.

On advancing from the wood, the Seaforths had to cross over a small ridge, then down into swampy ground and up a steeper incline into Wytschaete. Less than half way they encountered a new and thick barbed wire defence, with very few gaps, difficult to see in the darkening evening. Machine gun fire coming from North House began to cause casualties to the left-hand C Company as it negotiated this unwelcome obstacle, although German shooting was reported to be inaccurate and not as costly as it might have been. Until the afternoon this strong point had been held by a platoon of 1/East Yorks, but they had had to evacuate when it was shelled by British artillery. To their right, D Company veered off to their right, crossing the Vierstraat road and entering Wytschaete Wood. This had the unfortunate effect of dragging the support B and A

Companies with it, greatly weakening the main direction of attack on the village. The Seaforths now found themselves confronting several manned pillboxes that fought to the last: at one, on the outskirts of the village, Captain Reid and Company Sergeant Major Jeffries captured fourteen prisoners and five machine guns. North House continued to trouble the area north of Wytschaete until it was silenced and captured by 1/East Yorks and men of 3/39 Composite. Further south, the 1/Lincolns and 2/39 Composite also advanced and reached their first objective, a line from Peckham to Maedelstede Farm to the corner of Petit Bois, but could make no further progress.

During the night the three battalions of the South African Brigade, although now totalling no more than 650 men, joined the Seaforths as a welcome reinforcement in front of Wytschaete. The 4/SAI sent a detachment into the village; but it suffered losses from machine guns firing from pillboxes and was withdrawn.

During the afternoon, in a meeting held at Abbeville, Haig met with Foch and once again pressed him for reinforcements. He also urged the completion of a pre-planned sea water flooding of the Dunkirk area as a back-stop to any serious German breakthrough. The River Aa was already being flooded in the Dunkirk-Gravelines area. During the day a message was issued by Hamilton-Gordon at IX Corps headquarters to all the units under his command:

> 'The Commander-in-Chief has just been at Corps HQ. He would have liked to see all ranks now fighting on the Corps' front and tell each one of them of his personal appreciation of the magnificent fight they have made and are making. He would have liked to shake hands with each individual and thank him for what he has done. He has not time for this but has asked me to give everybody this message.'

Haig was right to be thankful for his men's efforts, for they had bought time – and the French reserves sent to Flanders by Foch were now arriving in force.

The French army begins to deploy in Flanders.
[Note that, for ease of reading, French *Divisions d'Infanterie* are referred to as DI, and *Regiments d'Infanterie* as RI.]
The first French formation to arrive was the 133DI, which reached Bergues as early as 12 April. Next day it was directed to Terdeghem, then Caestre. II Cavalry Corps arrived between Fauquembergues and La Ternoise on 13 April. Three days later it was assembled with two of its

divisions (the 2nd and 6th) north west of Steenvoorde and another (the 3rd) north of Cassel: this represented a considerable feat of management and endurance, for the Corps had covered 200-220 kilometres in the previous sixty hours, apparently with the loss of very few horses. Upon arrival, advanced and now dismounted elements of the Corps began to form a reserve line through Flêtre and St. Jans Cappel. 28DI took up a position on the left of II Cavalry Corps on the same day, completing a very long journey from Alsace, which included its trains coming under long-range shellfire at Amiens and Dunkirk.

Plumer had already made a local agreement with the commander of this force, Général Félix Robillot, for French units to relieve tired British units in the line. Foch would have none of it, citing his belief that this would serve only to paralyse both. The French would go into battle as properly formed formations, with their own known structures, methods and communications. Robillot's force would be held in reserve until this could be put into effect.

28DI was ordered to prepare the counter-attack towards Messines on 16 April (as already mentioned); but this essentially failed as the division was still arriving and simply could not fully deploy in the time given. Compelled by the urgency of the situation, units were thrown piecemeal

Kemmel had been a very pleasant village, in the lee of the great hill of Kemmelberg, with several large houses and the chateau. (Author)

Kemmel.-Het Kasteel.—Kemmel.-Le Château.

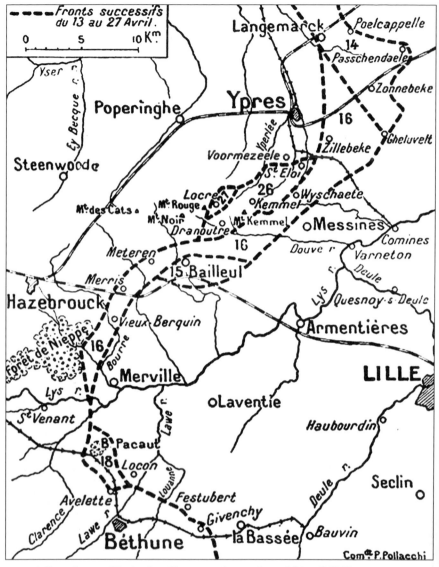

A French map, illustrating German gains made on 16 April 1918.

into battle, and suffered for it, just as all such local and exposed efforts had since the earliest days of the war. I Battalion of 22RI was first to go into action, under Captain Reynaud. At 8pm, the battalion began to move out from Kemmel, despite a violent bombardment falling on the area that lasted until 9.15pm. Under orders to advance to Messines, the battalion made some progress until it faced German resistance in the area of Spy Farm and D'Hoine Farm. Having broken through that, the advance continued; but it was brought to a standstill 200 metres short of Spanbroekmolen. Two attempts to attack there next morning met with no success, but by 4pm II Battalion had also arrived and the regiment was now holding a line from Lagache Farm to Spy Farm. Another attempt was made during the evening, with similar results, although I Battalion appears to have entered the German position at Spanbroekmolen and only been ejected after close fighting. The regiment's introduction to the Flanders front had cost it 120 men, including Reynaud, wounded, and young Lieutenant Louis Fausset-Crivelli, who died of multiple wounds sustained when leading the final charge. It proved to be only a portent of worse to come. As a consequence of such actions and the steady shellfire that fell on the area, 28DI had already lost twenty-five officers and 1024 men in the week or so since entering the line when the great German attack eventually came.

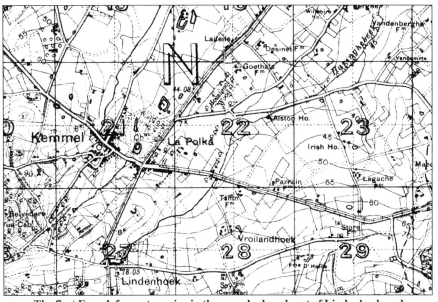

The first French forces to arrive in the area deployed east of Lindenhoek and La Polka, intending to advance on Spanbroekmolen.

Chapter Eight

Kemmelberg and the Flemish Hills

The first attack.
Fourth Army continued its attack on 17 April 1918, but met with an almost universal defeat of its ambitions. By the end of the day its corps were reporting that continuation of the offensive was impossible unless there could be relief by fresh divisions. Ironically, these reports were issued at much the same time that Foch and the British Chief of the Imperial General Staff, General Sir Henry Wilson, were seriously discussing abandoning Flanders and carrying out a further withdrawal.

The major effort by *Fourth Army*, known as Operation Tannenberg, falls outside the geographic scope of this book, for it fell on the Ypres Salient. It was soundly beaten off, notably by a wholly unexpected and vigorous counter-attack by Belgian forces at Merckem. The operation also met with failure in the area of Bailleul and Méteren. In the area on which this book is focused, it achieved virtually nothing except for a minor gain south of Kemmelberg at Donegal Farm and inflicting more losses to both sides.

At this point it would be useful to return to the topography of the battle. Having advanced westwards from Neuve Église, the Germans faced the line of Flemish Hills: on their right, the great double-summit bulk of Mont Kemmel (here usually referred to by its Flemish name, Kemmelberg, to avoid confusion with the village of Kemmel); and on the left, a little more distant, the peaks of Mont Noir, Mont Vidaigne and Mont Rouge. In between, the Neuve Église road ran through Dranoutre and ultimately up to the peak of the Scherpenberg behind it. In more peaceful times the area was, as it is today, a pleasant one for hikers and weekend tourists. At the top of the wooded Kemmelberg had stood a splendid, ornate, belvedere look-out tower, reached by walkers' footpaths, and the Belle Vue estaminet for the thirsty. Down on the western slope of the lesser of the two summits, which was known as Little Kemmel, stood Louis Windmill, and below that another refreshment stop, the Den Molen Cabaret. On the south east side, the hill of Great Kemmel sloped down to a small spur on which stood the crossroads hamlet of Lindenhoek, on the Neuve Église to Vierstraat road. The next crossroads north was at La Polka, which lay just east of the village of Kemmel.

Walkers might descend into the village, finding there its large church, chateau and grounds, and a pleasing grassy square, complete with obligatory bandstand. Long range shell fire and aerial bombing had laid waste to much of it by 1918. Below the heights, Kemmelberg was now riddled with tunnels and dugouts, with more in the lee of the hill on the northern side.

German possession of these heights was an objective of Operation Georgette, enabling domination of the supply railway coming up from Hazebrouck through Godewaersvelde to Poperinge; the road coming into the same area from Steenvoorde; and much of the area used for the camps, stores and artillery for the Ypres Salient. Once the hills were in German hands, continued British occupation of Ypres was at least seriously endangered; at worst, it would be rendered impossible. The hills were now tantalisingly close. The summit of Kemmelberg was only 1600 metres ahead of the nearest German lines, the hill sloping steeply upwards and filling the horizon behind the British defences.

Fourth Army's approach was to outflank Kemmelberg rather than face the prospect of frontal attack, which was considered too difficult. The main weight of the attack was therefore assembled to aim at the gentler ground towards Dranoutre and the less intimidating westward slopes. It would face a very mixed British force: on the German left, covering Dranoutre, was the composite battalion made up of what had been 100 Brigade and another improvised unit known as Wyatt's Force after its temporary commander, Brigadier General Louis Wyatt.

Brigadier General Louis Wyatt organised an improvised defence force covering the approach to Kemmelberg. (Author)

Consisting of sappers of the Royal Engineer field companies of the 25th Division, men of 9/Loyal North Lancashire and various details from Second Army and VI Corps Schools, this unit straddled the Dranoutre – Neuve Église road. Its ability to fight effectively was limited: the Royal Engineers' would later write that they had no rifle or hand grenades, no flares or rockets, no form of visual signalling, no method of communication with the artillery, and that message runners had to cross four kilometres of shell-swept ground to headquarters. Next to Wyatt's Force came the 2/6 Sherwood Foresters of 178 Brigade, which was now incorporated into the structure of the 19th (Western) Division. The junction between the two near Donegal Farm was a weak point, as such inter-divisional boundaries inevitably were. Things were not helped when the Foresters discovered a wide gap between them and Wyatt's men, and had to call upon a platoon of 2/5th Sherwood Foresters to help fill it. Whether by good intelligence or sheer luck, the German attack enjoyed one of its few successes in the area of the junction. Behind it, the three battalions of 71 Brigade were in reserve near Dranoutre and were already aware that French reinforcements were now not far away.

At 6.25am the German bombardment began, falling on the area held by 74 and 103 Brigades, as well as 100 (Composite) Brigade and Wyatt's Force, in front of Hille and Dranoutre. The shells searched to and fro behind the lines and also concentrated on the newly dug trenches. Casualties were heavy, especially in 100 Brigade, which was already at a very low ebb in terms of available manpower. An attack shaping up against 103 Brigade at 8.30am was stopped in its tracks by British artillery. Three more, all made against 74 Brigade during the day, met with the same fate. There would be no German troops advancing through Dranoutre on this day, except for the deserters and captured. Two prisoners of *Thüringisches Infanterie-Regiment 71 (38th Division)*, captured by Glasgow Highlanders, let it slip that their regiment was massed for an attack that was due to start at 8.10am, but nothing seemed to happen on the front of 100 Brigade until some time later. Just as Major John Chalmers was obtaining information, relieving the prisoners of some very useful maps, a Very light gun and an automatic pistol, he was killed by a shell. Chalmers was one of six brothers, three of whom lost their lives in the war.

One company, just a hundred men strong, of 6/7th Highland Light Infantry now arrived from 178 Brigade and was placed at the disposal of 100 Brigade, for it had no other reserve on which it could call if the expected attack did come. And it did: by 12.20pm the Glasgow Highlanders were having to report that the enemy had forced a lodgement in the centre of its line, in an orchard north of Keersebrom. The line there had been destroyed in the bombardment and German infantry had occupied the wasteland. They could advance no further as the battalion kept them pinned down by rifle and Lewis gun fire, but neither could they retire. The Highlanders were given permission to use the 6/7th Highland Light Infantry in order to carry out a counter attack, but it soon broke down – not least as its only two officers had become casualties on the way up. Another attempt was made at 6.30pm after a fifteen-minute bombardment of the lodgement, but this time the three companies of 5/York & Lancaster Regiment could make no more progress than had the earlier attempt. One cannot help but admire the tenacity of the small

104

German garrison. Gradually, an effective defensive line of posts was created all around the British side of the lodgement, and it was effectively ignored.

Kemmelberg stood behind the almost five kilometres of front held by the 19th (Western) Division. This was a strong position, with a continuous and wired front line trench, behind which was a position made up of part-trenches and pillboxes forming a support line. Some of this was the old 'GHQ Line', which had been dug across the southern slope of Kemmelberg in earlier years. The line enjoyed good observation and fields of fire across to the German front, which was now on ground that sloped gradually down to the infant Douve.

The divisional area came under shell and gas bombardment, which seemed to concentrate more on the hill than on the front line area. Reports vary regarding the start time, from 4.30am to 7am, suggesting that the shelling was not universally applied to the whole area. The buried signal cable network was destroyed and the deep-reaching shellfire meant that ground telephone lines could only be run out as far as Brulooze, meaning that all messages in front of, on, and behind Kemmelberg would have to be by runner. German infantry was seen massing, notably over the crest at Lindenhoek, but British counter-preparation artillery fire held off any serious attack until about 10.35am. Many reports talk of small parties of Germans 'trickling forward' while the two sets of artillery were blazing away.

Across most of the front of 178, 56 and 57 Brigades, the German infantry was pinned down at a distance of 4-500 metres by intense small arms and machine gun fire, and barrages from British and also now French artillery. The attackers also endured a day of frequent aerial bombing and strafing, for the Royal Air Force had long since achieved almost complete air superiority in this battle. Despite this resistance and the tactical advantages of the British position, it was almost inevitable, given the weight of attack, that the line would give somewhere. It took place in the area of Donegal Farm, the weak junction between 178 Brigade and Wyatt's Force, and Germans seized the farm itself. The 1/Leicesters of 71 Brigade, in reserve, reported men falling back from the front line, just south of the farm, under shell fire. Its B Company, positioned not far behind the line, sent the stragglers back again and two of the company's platoons went forward to reinforce them at the front. Two battalions of the French 99RI of 28DI were also ordered from reserve to assist in the defence and recovery of Donegal Farm.

At 6pm the French battalions attempted a counter-attack to regain the farm, but were beaten back by machine gun fire. They did, however, succeed after two further attempts during the night. In doing so, they found the bodies of Second Lieutenant Arthur Garrett and five sappers of 456 Field Company RE. They had been with a party of twelve who had been sent to defend Donegal Farm. French reports suggested that the sappers had put up a stern fight, for some fifty German dead were also found there.

At around the same time that the French were engaged at Donegal Farm, *Fourth Army's* Chief of Staff, General Fritz von Lossberg, put a call through to General Hermann von Kuhl, his opposite number at *Crown Prince Rupprecht's Army Group* headquarters. He explained that all of his divisions were now exhausted and in need of urgent relief, and that they were now clinging onto a tactically disadvantageous position in front of Kemmelberg. Von Kuhl regretted that he had no reserves to offer, but the situation might change favourably if an attack being made by the Guard Corps at Ypres next day made good progress. It did not. There was now no option. 'Georgette' was closed down and the decision was made that efforts would be concentrated down on the Somme, with an attack in the area of Villers-Bretonneux. The force in Flanders would be restructured before any further major attempt would be made.

During the evening of 17 April, a party of Germans approached to within a hundred metres of the 2/6th Sherwood Foresters. On being discovered and fired upon, the party withdrew, leaving in place an officer who persisted in sniping through the night. In broad daylight the next morning, Second Lieutenant Robert Jackson went out alone and captured him. Jackson, who had won the Distinguished Conduct Medal when serving in the ranks of the West Yorkshire Regiment in 1916, was now awarded the Military Cross. The two citations provide insight into his character:

'With one man he attacked about seventy of the enemy, throwing bombs at them and causing many casualties' (DCM) and 'Throughout heavy fighting lasting for four days this officer displayed great courage and devotion to duty, setting a fine example to his men. Largely owing to his initiative a determined enemy attack was on one occasion defeated, and in another instance he captured an enemy officer who was harassing our line by sniping, going out in broad daylight under heavy artillery and machine-gun fire and making him a prisoner.' (MC).

He was killed in action, aged just 22, on 23 October 1918.

Regrouping and rethinking.
On 17 April the various French divisions now in Flanders were organised

into a command to be known as the Détachement d'Armée du Nord (DAN), placed under the orders of Général Antoine de Mitry. Foch now issued a directive to Robillot and Plumer:

'The important things are:
1. To assure at all costs the occupation of the 'massif' Kemmel - Mont Noir - Mont des Cats, not forgetting to watch the direction Dickebusch - Ypres.
2. To extend the ground already occupied by capturing the lower slopes of the 'massif' and, if it be possible, the higher ground on which the enemy is established, such as Neuve Église, Wytschaete and Bailleul.
3. With this object in view, the proper course is to proceed to attacks each aimed at an objective relatively close, which should then be organized as a base for a fresh attack on a fresh objective. For this purpose: concentration of artillery fire, relatively little infantry.
4. These offensive actions should be begun without delay, in order to profit from the activity of our troops and not to allow the enemy time to reorganise.
5. On principle, always keep in reserve one French [infantry] division and one French cavalry division.
6. All British troops withdrawn from the battle should be reorganised close behind it, so as to be available to support or relieve the troops in front in case of need.'

German intentions.

Despite OHL giving instructions on 20 April to close down the Flanders offensive, it left open the idea of carrying out further attacks at Givenchy (deep in *Sixth Army's* area) and at Kemmelberg. A preliminary operation to capture the Lindenhoek spur was mooted, but abandoned in favour of the main attack being slightly earlier in that area, to capture it so that it would provide no further nuisance. Offensive operations east of Ypres were also closed down and three divisions (*13th Reserve, 19th Reserve and 233rd*) were moved to reinforce and refresh the force for the Kemmelberg attack. The date was set for 25 April.

The frontage of the attack would be from Haegedoorne to the Ypres-Comines canal. A first advance would be made to secure a line from Haegedoorne, round the north side of Dranoutre, to the Kemmelbeek and thence to the southern end of the Dickebusch reservoir. To achieve this would mean capturing Dranoutre, all of Kemmelberg, Kemmel itself and all of the British Vierstraat and Cheapside Lines. In other words, an audacious and very demanding objective. Once that had been achieved, converging attacks on the west and east of the front would reach the line Vlamertinghe to Brandhoek to Reninghelst, which meant capturing Scherpenberg and much of the area of La Clytte, Dickebusch and Ouderdom occupied by so much British artillery, so many camps and the war materiel supporting the Ypres front. If that was achieved, the continued British ability to hold Ypres was doomed.

Twelve divisions were assembled for the operation. On the right, *XVIII Reserve Corps* would tackle the area from Lindenhoek northwards and employ (right to left) *7, 13 Reserve, 19 Reserve and 56 Divisions* in the front line. *X Reserve Corps* was confronted with the task of capturing Dranoutre and Kemmelberg, using the *Alpine Corps, 4 Bavarian and 22 Reserve Divisions*: the first two were known to be first-class fighting formations with a strong track record; *22 Reserve* was rated by the Allies as a much less formidable foe.

The French deployment.
French units now relieved almost all of the British between Lagache Farm and 3 Australian Brigade, which was now holding the line to the north east of Méteren. Four divisions took over the front. South to north they were: 133DI, which faced Bailleul (which meant that it was outside the proposed area of German attack); 34DI, which led up as far as the River Douve near Dranoutre; 154DI, holding Dranoutre and along the Donegal Farm road to Aircraft Farm; and 28DI, on the line in front of Kemmelberg on the Lindenhoek spur. Held in reserve were 39DI and the three divisions of II Cavalry Corps, as well as assorted British units still in the rear of the area. The 9th (Scottish) Division took the line up from there to the woods near Wytschaete and looped around a salient to St Eloi; the 21st Division and the 6th Division took the line on to and beyond the Ypres-Comines canal.

The Kemmelberg position was a difficult one, despite the obvious advantage of observation. The front line was close in to the slopes, giving no depth or room for manoeuvre. The forward zone was therefore much compressed, and the trenches and dugouts of Kemmelberg were, in retrospect, very over-manned, leaving too little in reserve for counter-attack and exposing these concentrations of men to the devastating shellfire they would inevitably face.

At 9am on the evening of 24 April, II and III Battalions of 30RI (28DI) undertook an attack to push its line forward at Lindenhoek, intending to reach the line from Daylight Corner to the old Kingsway communication trench and on to Frenchman's Farm. It met with stiff resistance from enemy machine guns and was not helped by the French

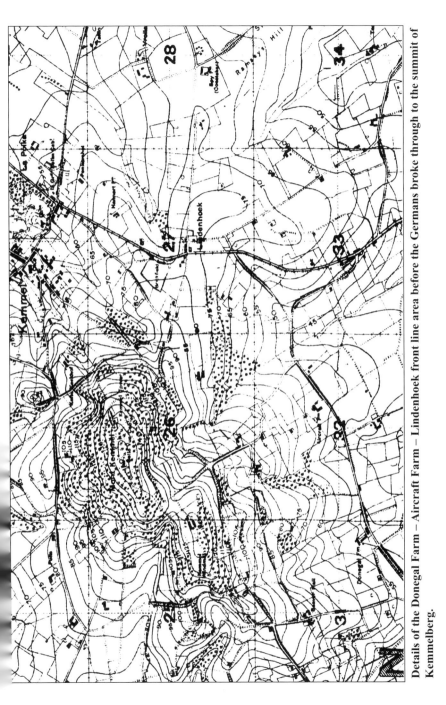

Details of the Donegal Farm – Aircraft Farm – Lindenhoek front line area before the Germans broke through to the summit of Kemmelberg.

From almost anywhere on the battlefield, Kemmelberg hill is a dominant feature. (Author)

artillery firing short, causing casualties to the attacking troops. The regiment gained only perhaps 250 metres, and was still in the process of digging-in and reorganising when the German attack struck. A prisoner taken by 416RI told of an impending large scale attack with gas, and tell-tale sounds of movement were heard, but no aerial reconnaissance had suggested anything serious was about to take place.

25 April: Inferno at Kemmelberg.
The early phase of the German attack began at 2.30am with the by-now familiar intensive and deep artillery bombardment, with much phosgene and lachrymatory gas, on the Allied artillery and communications. In all, 290 artillery batteries, of which 128 were heavy or super-heavy, were in action simultaneously. In the French area, many of these batteries fired over the Kemmelberg massif in order to hit the gun batteries located on the northern side. Witnesses would report that virtually all of the French artillery was neutralised if not destroyed, with barely one gun per battery being able to remain in action. Once again, this all took place on a foggy morning, making visibility very poor and rendering men who were forced to don their respirators all but blind to their surroundings. French reports were that the fire was extremely heavy, not experienced since Verdun, and one commentator called Kemmelberg a 'tempest of fire'. Within a short time, most of the forward telephone lines had been cut; machine gun posts were destroyed; men dead or dazed. Between 5 and 6am the

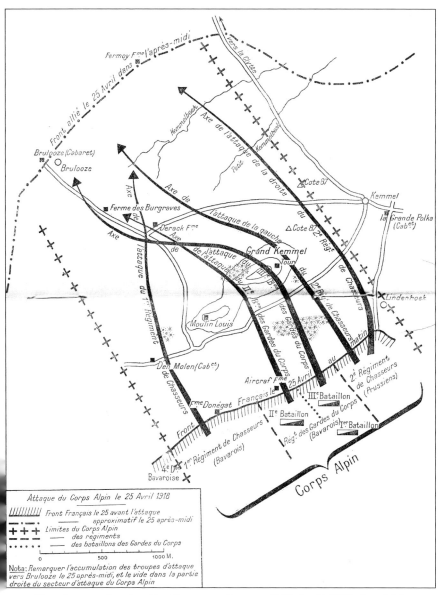

French map showing the German advance of 25 April 1918, in which Kemmelberg was captured and progress made towards the Scherpenberg.

continuous bombardment ceased, becoming interrupted and with only occasional teasing bursts of fire, before switching to the front line positions, at which point the trench mortars joined in the destruction. 30RI war diary notes,

'A very violent artillery fires on our lines and at our backs ... A considerable number of new batteries came into action ... At 5:30am the front line and support trenches are entirely levelled, some sections [of our men] are almost wiped out at their battle position.'

They would very soon be joined by a massive concentration of some 318 aircraft, employed to bomb and machine gun at low level. Men who had lived through the opening hours of 'Michael' or 'Georgette' would readily recognise the regiment's plight. At one point, the wind appeared to blow the phosgene back towards the German troops massing in the Douve valley; but it seems to have had little effect on the forthcoming attack.

The Alpine Corps had been given the toughest job of all, not only to overcome the first French lines but to capture Kemmelberg by outflanking it on either side. The steep slope ahead of them, daunting enough to today's walker or cyclist, was a distinct physical challenge; but we must recall that this was a formation of picked men, trained and recently used to operating in the mountains of the Dolomites. Even so, they were well prepared, carrying four days' supplies and all of the ammunition and equipment one would expect of a formation given such a task. On the left, *Bayerische Jäger Regiment 1* would tackle Donegal Farm before advancing on through Den Molen Cabaret and the western side of Little Kemmel behind it, held by 416RI; next to them came *Bayerische Infanterie Leib Regiment.* Its II Battalion would advance past Aircraft Farm to the col between Little and Greater Kemmel, at the junction between 416RI and 30RI, while the III Battalion went directly for the peak of Great Kemmel. On the right, *Jäger Regiment 2* would break through 30RI at Lindenhoek and pass around the eastern side of Great Kemmel. On the German left, *4 Bavarian Infanterie-Division* deployed its three regiments to attack Dranoutre and advance towards Locre, opposed by 413RI.

At 5.45am on the left and 6am on the right, the firing switched to a creeping barrage behind which the German infantry could advance. The fifteen minute difference was to allow for *56 Infanterie-Division* to capture the Lindenhoek – Vroilandhoek plateau before the *Alpine Corps* and *4 Bavarian Infanterie-Division* on their left rose to join them in the assault. Within the morning these formations carved three serious breaches in the defences and were well on their way to their objectives: it was possibly the most serious moment for the British force in France since the peak of the First Battle of Ypres in 1914. One commentator uses the metaphor of the French drowning in the flood of the German assault.

Moving through the French defences with remarkable speed, infantry of *III/Bayerische Infanterie Leib Regiment* stood on the summit of Great Kemmel by 8.10am. Many of the French reserves in support dugouts, having been pinned down by the intense shellfire, were simply washed over and killed or captured before being able to move. Trench mortars and German flamethrower detachments overcame points of more stubborn resistance. Within another half an hour the village of Kemmel was also in German hands, and by now well over 2000 Frenchmen had been taken prisoner.

Jäger Regiment 2 advanced to within 200m of the summit of Little Kemmel, using the cover of a sunken lane behind Aircraft Farm, whose garrison had been killed by the shellfire. II Battalion of 416IR, which had been held in reserve just over the hill, carried out two counter-attacks in an attempt to hold the hill but without success and at great cost. All resistance by units holding Little Kemmel was reduced and eliminated, in a situation that had rapidly become impossible

Jean Louis Camille Bec, a cyclist with 416RI, served at Kemmelberg and was one of only 755 of 2550 of his regiment to survive the battle. He earned the Croix de Guerre at Verdun and the Médaille Militaire for his part in the battle in April 1918. (Europeana)

for the defenders, as it also now came under fire from enemy troops on Great Kemmel, and now in flank by *Jäger Regiment 2 Reserve*, which had advanced to the west of Donegal Farm and turned inward. The final resistance appears to have been overcome by around 11.45am; but Allied intelligence continued to believe that friendly troops were on the hill throughout the afternoon, and so there was a natural reluctance to fire on it.

It was, by any measure, an incredible military achievement. The geographic bastion of defence and the best point of observation in Flanders had fallen within half a day, and along with it 8200 prisoners, fifty-three artillery pieces and 233 machine guns.

The 19/Lancashire Fusiliers, which in earlier days had been recognisable as the 3rd Salford Pals, was one of the British units in the rear of the French defences when Kemmelberg fell. A pioneer battalion to the 49th (West Riding) Division, it had been working in company shifts for several days, digging a 2500 metres communication trench from Kemmelberg to the Scherpenberg. Under regular shellfire, it had lost men steadily during the previous days, but 25 April was to prove disastrous. B Company was out digging when the German bombardment began at

Mont "Kemmel" Belgique
Mai 1918

This French soldier was certainly not at Kemmelberg in May 1918. His dugout is more likely to have been at the Scherpenberg, Hyde Park Corner or even further away at Mont Noir or Mont Rouge. (Europeana)

2.30pm, and suffered badly while it continued to work and later on, when German infantry streamed towards it from over the summit. Battalion headquarters and the companies that were resting were located in dugouts and tunnels on the north hill face. They attempted to join in the defence of the hill's east side, but were outflanked and surrounded as *Jäger Regiment 2* broke through 30DI. By day's end, the battalion had lost fourteen officers and 333 men, many of whom were taken prisoner.

Among them was the commanding officer, Lieutenant Colonel J. Ambrose Smith, captured after being wounded in the shoulder. Also taken into captivity was Lieutenant Colonel Hugh Bousfield, commanding the improvised Kemmel Hill Defence Force, who was awarded the French Croix de Guerre for his work in assisting the defence of Kemmelberg during 17 April.

With the summits secured and with *Fourth Army* having given confirmation orders to continue the attack, the Alpine Corps paused at the Kemmelbeek stream (sometimes called the Vijverbeek) before pushing onwards, continuing its advance behind a creeping barrage. On making the descent on the north side, *III/Bayerische Infanterie Leib Regiment* lost direction and veered badly to its left, taking it towards Burgrave Farm and Brulooze, on the way to the Scherpenberg. At the same time, *Jäger Regiment 1* tended to move to its right, which meant that the two forces were converging. This naturally concentrated large numbers of troops going in the direction of Brulooze but left the right hand side of the attack, going towards Fermoy Farm and La Clytte, much weakened.

Behind the pioneers, the 19th (Western) Divisional artillery was under the command of Brigadier General William Monkhouse and situated around Brulooze and Fermoy Farm in front of the Scherpenberg. Monkhouse would later recall,

'The Germans actually arrived among the guns of 87th and 88th Brigades [RFA] before they could be seen and my men took them on hand to hand, and in some of the batteries removed the breech blocks and were able to hide them so as to prevent the Germans from using them. … An airman flew over us and dropped a message, "We have retaken Kemmel". By this time the fog had cleared.

I could see the top of the hill covered in French soldiers. It appears that when the Germans attacked the French got into the tunnel that had been made for observation posts through the hill. The Germans drove them out and stuck them on top of the hill to prevent our shooting at it. Arrived back at French divisional HQ I reported "Mon Général, Kemmel est perdu". With his head in his hands he remarked "Mon Général, c'est un accident, mais ce n'est pas – pas un accident – très grave"! As from the top of the hill one could see the coast from Ostende to Dunkirk I agreed to differ.'

That German troops had reached the gun positions indicates how thoroughly they had broken the Kemmelberg defences. By day's end, they had advanced their line to within a short distance of Locre and the Scherpenberg and the Kaiser was proclaiming victory: but on the right, although an advance had been made, the attack had failed to secure the objective of the British Cheapside Line and French reserves had now moved to hold the line from Locre, past the Scherpenberg to La Clytte.

25 April: from Kemmel to the Ypres-Comines Canal.
The 9th (Scottish) Division was still holding six kilometres of front line when the German attack commenced. Although it had not faced any serious attack since 17 April, the men had been under great strain due to incessant shellfire and casualties, particularly in the support lines, had been numerous. The division now had its own 27 Brigade on the right next to the French, positioned between Lagache Farm and Black Cot, north of Wytschaete Wood. From there, it had temporary command of 146 Brigade (normally 49th Division) which carried the line on to North House; then 64 Brigade (21st Division) from there to Dome House, where the Dammstrasse meets the St. Eloi to Oosttaverne road. Finally on the division's left flank, its own 26 Brigade carried the line on to Eikhof Farm, not far from the Ypres-Comines canal. Behind the front line, it also had control of the Vierstraat and Cheapside reserve lines. The South African Brigade was in the process of reorganising. The division was also strengthened by the arrival of thirteen Lewis gun sections from 5th Battalion Tank Corps, which had been set up at Vandamme Hill, north west of Petit Bois.

The great German bombardment opened on the division's area at 2.30am, just as it did on the French. French SOS signals were seen, and all telephone communications with 27 Brigade were soon destroyed. The first that divisional headquarters heard that any infantry attack was taking place came at 7.15am – and it was most concerning, for it was the artillery reporting that enemy troops were at Siege Farm, which was behind the Vierstraat Line and some two kilometres behind the 12/Royal Scots, which had been holding the flank at Lagache Farm. Ominously, there had been no word from them.

Behind the infantry, the British artillery, much of which had recently remained silent in order to preserve the secrecy of its location, suffered from the German bombardment its worst day of the war in terms of casualties per battery.

The 12/Royal Scots' experience mirrored that of many units in recent fighting. Under immense bombardment, in gas and fog, and with no communications possible as all message runners were never seen again, it had the shortest of notice when enemy infantry began their attack at 5.30am. For a while the battalion's Lewis guns and rifle fire kept the

Germans at arm's length, but at almost the same time that it was realised that the French were no longer in evidence on the right, enemy troops began to envelope the rear of the battalion's position from that direction. The fight continued until about 8.30am, when those who could began to retire and cut through to the support lines. On finding parts of the Vierstraat Line already held by Germans, the withdrawal continued until it reached the second, the Cheapside Line. When the roll call was finally taken, it was found that the battalion had lost 559 officers and men, of whom 502 were simply missing. Only eighty-eight were still with the battalion. It is now known that on this day alone 107 men lost their lives. Several of them were aged 18 and had been with the battalion only a matter of days; seven were more seasoned and experienced men whose loss would be keenly felt, for they had already been awarded Military Medals for bravery. Among them, Private 43346 Andrew Neill from Mochrum in Wigtownshire, was the third of three brothers to be killed in the war.

A very large proportion of those who lost their lives in the battle have no known, identified, grave today. (Author)

The Germans pressed on, dealing with 6/King's Own Scottish Borderers, who had been holding the reserve Vierstraat Line from York

House to the crossroads at Vierstraat. The battalion's war diary, never one noted for its verbosity, merely says 'Enemy attack. Headquarters, B and D Companies surrounded and cut off'. Its two reserve companies, which had been at Siege Farm, followed previous orders to retire to man a line from Beaver Corner to the Willebeke stream, and did so with few casualties. They came in contact with 9/KOYLI on their left but found no sign of any Allied troops to the right. Beyond a gap, *56 Infanterie-Division*, which had already captured Kemmel, was pushing on towards La Clytte. The KOSB's precarious position was eased by the movement of 11/Royal Scots, 8/Black Watch and 9/Durham Light Infantry (DLI) into the area and, although the German advance had taken it some way along the Milky Way track towards Millekruise, no further attack on the 9th (Scottish) Division's right flank took place. The KOSB is even reported to have carried out a small counter-attack and to have taken fifty-eight prisoners.

In the centre of the division's front in the Wytschaete area, the *19 Reserve-Infanterie Division* and *13 Reserve-Division* made slow progress, held up by determined but costly resistance.

The first that the headquarters of 1/East Yorks knew that an infantry attack had commenced was when some small parties of Germans were spotted wandering over the ridge into the eastern side of Grand Bois. Not a word had come from its front line companies. Two small headquarters detachments were formed, which kept any more Germans at bay by sniping. Gradually, machine guns came into action from Petit Bois and Wytschaete Wood, and the detachments had no choice but to withdraw. Eventually, two junior officers, the Medical Officer and thirty men made it to the safety of the Cheapside Line. Of the front line companies in the area of Onraet Wood, which had been enveloped after being subjected to trench mortar fire, flamethrower attack and smoke barrage, barely a man escaped.

Next to the East Yorks, the 1/5th West Yorks (146 Brigade) held the line from Black Cot to North House, across the north west face of Wytschaete. As the bombardment rained down, no information came from its front line companies. Runners, sent from battalion headquarters to find out what was going on, came back at 6.40am with the disconcerting news that C Company of the 1/6th West Yorks was fighting a rearguard action on the left at Zero Wood (just north of Onraet Wood and some 400 metres behind the battalion's front line); but other information was vague and no contact could be made with the 1/East Yorks. Two of the battalion's reserve platoons were ordered to form a defence between Grand Bois and Bois Quarante, which did enough to hold off enemy incursions while a withdrawal was made in the Vierstraat direction and a position was taken up in Chinese Trench. Gradually through the day, with no or conflicting information but much evidence that Germans were massing around Vandamme Farm, a withdrawal was made through Vierstraat to the Cheapside Line.

The 1/6th West Yorks suffered from the same, sad depletion of its front line garrisons during the shelling, and the same problems of communication and intelligence during the morning. C Company, which was holding out at Zero Wood, had the unusual distinction of being commanded by an officer whose tunic was adorned by the riband of the Victoria Cross: Captain George Sanders, a Leeds man who had been decorated for his work at the Schwaben Redoubt at the beginning of the Battle of the Somme in 1916. A runner, reporting to battalion headquarters, reported that he had last seen Sanders rallying his men while standing on a concrete pillbox and firing at the enemy with his revolver at a range of just twenty metres. Despite being shot in the arm and leg, Sanders continued in action until he was taken as a notable prisoner of war, surrounded by a German machine gun detachment.

Just after noon, *73 Reserve-Infanterie-Regiment* of *19 Reserve-Division* captured the Vierstraat crossroads as the various British units withdrew towards the Cheapside Line.

Further north, towards the Dammstrasse, it appears that the German *7 Infanterie-Division* failed to employ the proven, successful tactics of small parties, speed and infiltration but instead advanced in masses. The 7/Seaforths, in the area of Piccadilly Farm and Bois Quarante, and 5/Cameron Highlanders beyond them, came under heavy attack but managed to create a flank on their right. The action of these two Scots units, which gave way here and there but essentially held, ensured there would be no northward-turning movement against Ypres.

The 5/Camerons held the line from Eikhof Farm to Dome House at the end of the Dammstrasse, keeping two companies in near support at the Mound near St Eloi. The battalion's diary recalls that 'HE, shrapnel and gas shells came over like rain' between 3am and 6am, and that casualties, particularly to the headquarters detachment, were considerable. When the German infantry began to attack and a serious threat to the right flank became apparent, headquarters moved to the far (western) side of St Eloi, to Bus House. The battalion's machine gun and rifle fire, supported by the Vickers guns of a company of 9 Machine Gun Battalion, kept the enemy at bay at other parts of its front, but steps had to be taken to pull back on the right-hand end; this came into contact with 7/Seaforths near Bois Confluent. The volumes of fire being poured into the German ranks soon used up the battalion's local stocks of ammunition. 'Several men, with absolute disregard of personal danger, went forward a distance of 150m and brought back Small Arms Ammunition from dumps which had been vacated. Thus heavily laden, they made this hazardous journey several times … subjected to extremely heavy machine gun fire.' The diary does not reveal how many of the forty-four men who lost their lives this day did so while carrying out this selfless act.

For two hours, from 11.30am, the battalion's position and the whole area of St Eloi and the Mound came under renewed, intensive and relentless shelling. The front posts continued to hold on, but losses inevitably mounted until in some cases they were 'knocked out to a man'. Gradually, the two forward companies (A and B) that had been holding the outpost line were practically annihilated, leaving the other two companies that had been holding the line from Piccadilly Farm to the Mound to become the new front line. Pressure grew as it became evident that the Germans were making progress on the left, against 2/39 Composite Battalion. Orders that had been given by brigade for the battalion to carry out a withdrawal to Voormezele did not arrive, and in the event the ever-reducing garrison held on until about 8.15pm, when it withdrew to around Bus House. The battalion had lost seven officers and 247 men.

On their left, the 2/39 Composite Battalion had come into the line and held it between Eikhof Farm and the Spoil Bank on the Ypres-Comines canal. It too came under heavy shellfire; but the German infantry attack fell principally on its right-hand B Company. One platoon is described as being annihilated; the other fell back through Triangle Wood. Eventually a flank was formed, first to Shelly Farm and later to Bus House.

The end of the day saw the British front line now running from south east of La Clytte, to the Cheapside Line at the Willebeek and on to Ridge Wood. It then crossed forward to the Vierstraat Line and followed it to Voormezele and thence to Bus House.

The attack against the British had, therefore, made some territorial gains but fallen far short of its ultimate goal, and not even achieved its initial objective. Sixt von Arnim's *Fourth Army* headquarters was also beginning to receive intelligence reports of large-scale Allied troops movements; almost certainly the arrival of two extra French divisions in the area near to the Channel coast. Even so, a decision was made for the attack to be renewed at 8am on 26 April. During the night, as if to remind the Allies that the Germans were still more than capable, sixteen tons of bombs were dropped from the air on Poperinge.

As the situation became clearer during the day, both in terms of the weather and the situation in the French zone, any reserves to hand had

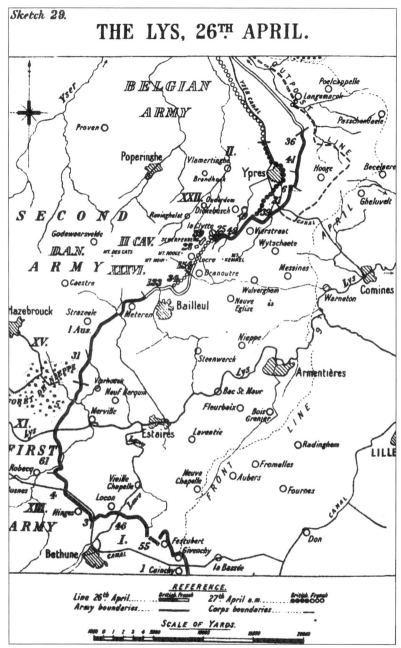

A map from the British Official History, showing the Allied front line at the end of the Battle of the Lys.

been ordered into position: they included mounted troops, cyclists and motor machine gun units. They would play a part in ensuring that there would be no further German progress beyond the Cheapside Line. But there were also larger plans being made: Generals de Mitry and Plumer agreed to carry out a large-scale counter-attack, employing the fresh and rested French 39DI and the tattered British 25th Division. Had they been aware that, by the afternoon, German units were becoming exhausted by their efforts and depleted by casualties and that a cautious OHL was already preparing to call off the Flanders offensive, their spirits would rightfully have been high.

A postcard view of the completely razed ground of Kemmel and the surrounding area. (Author)

26 April and later.

The Allied attempt to counter-attack proved to be a fiasco of poor staff work and co-ordination, insufficient artillery support and general dislocation. Robillot and Plumer had originally agreed to strike at 5pm on 25 April, but this proved to be terribly optimistic. The 39DI was still moving into the area and could not be in position on time, and Robillot's orders for the 25th Division (which had been placed under his command in an effort to properly co-ordinate the attack) did not arrive until 3.30pm. The whole affair was postponed until 3am next day. And then it rained: it rained in torrents, flooding the Kemmelbeek and rendering the already-ravaged ground a quagmire.

The collection of artillery gathered for the operation did not remotely provide the weight of fire upon which such operations now relied and only through which they could succeed. In particular, it was very short of heavy howitzers, with an average of just one for every hundred metres of line to be attacked. The opening bombardment, aimed at the line of the Kemmelbeek, which was set as the first infantry objective, proved to be so feeble that the Germans did not recognise it as a sign of a forthcoming attack but only as normal harassing fire. Beyond the Kemmelbeek, the infantry would advance behind a creeping barrage, initially at a hundred metres every four minutes, slowing to ten minutes as the final objective was approached. For the 39DI, that final objective was the very front line from which the French had been ejected the previous day: in many ways, not least due to the short time for preparation and the ground conditions, this represented a more stretching goal than that which had been given to the *Alpine Corps*. It was never going to work, and 39DI knew it. Arriving at their un-reconnoitred start positions wet through, in the dark night and after a very lengthy approach march, the division did not begin to advance until half an hour after the time that had been set. It immediately met with volumes of German machine gun and artillery fire, and really only consolidated the line already held, pushing it slightly further from the Scherpenberg.

That the 39DI did not advance caused a serious problem for the 25th Division, for it had made good progress and in pushing well forward through Kemmel was now exposed to fire from both flanks. It was obliged to retire back to the line of the Kemmelbeek, which did at least mean that a net gain had been made, but at terrible and wholly unnecessary cost.

The counter-attack had been made, right to left, by 74 and 7 brigades. In the dark, wet and with only the thin artillery bombardment, it achieved surprise and made rapid progress, despite the now heavy ground that caused the attackers to fall behind the protective creeping barrage. As dawn came, the attack was also masked by fog. The 74 Brigade attacked using the 3/Worcester and 9/Loyal North Lancashire, which moved ahead well from its start line between Le Clytte and Millekruise but found the steep-sided Kemmelbeek to be more of a barrier than they had anticipated. Once that was overcome, enemy machine guns beyond were rushed and captured with few losses. More resistance was met at RE Farm; but this was also dealt with and the battalions, increasingly mixed up in the fog, entered Kemmel. Fighting through it house by house, the brigade pushed past the chateau and some hundred metres into open country beyond the village. By this time casualties were mounting. 7 Brigade, on their left, employing 10/Cheshires and 4/South Staffords, with 1/Wilts in close support, also reached Kemmel but sustained casualties that included all three battalion commanders. By 8am it had become all too clear that units on either side were not keeping up, and the counter-attack was abandoned; the units withdrew to the line of a light railway in front of La Clytte.

The British at home were kept remarkably well-informed of progress. For example, the *Sheffield Daily Telegraph* of 27 April included the text of a German communiqué:

'GERMANY. Friday Night. Enemy counter-attacks against Kemmelberg ... failed, with heavy losses. Friday Afternoon Western theatre: The attack by the army of General Sixt von Arnim against Kemmelberg led to a complete success. The height itself, looking far into the Flanders plain, is in our possession. Yesterday morning, after strong artillery activity, the infantry of General Sieger and General von Eberhardt broke forward to the attack. French divisions entrusted, within the radius of the British troops. with the defence of Kemmelberg and the English troops adjoining them at Wytschaete and Dranoutre, were thrown out of their positions. The large crater of St. Eloi and the place itself were captured. The numerous concrete houses and fortified farms situated in the fighting area were captured. Prussian and Bavarian troops took Kemmelberg and the village by storm. Under the protection of the artillery, which keeps up with our troops in spite of the difficult terrain, the infantry pushed forward at many points as far as the Kemmelbeek. We captured Dranoutre and the height to the north-west of Vleugelhoek. Battle squadrons [of aircraft] attacked with great success the rear communication roads of the enemy, which were crowded with carts and columns. As a result of yesterday's battle over 6,500 prisoners have been reported up to the present, the majority of whom are French. Among the prisoners are one English and one French regimental commander.'

The chilling significance of this news would have been well understood by the many British and Dominion troops who were in hospital or in training at the time. But they would be unaware that not all was proceeding according to German plan, for 26 April would also prove to be a most disappointing day for the Germans. On the left, *4 Bavarian Infanterie-Division* attacked the French 154DI in the Locre area but made scant progress. After hours of close quarter fighting, with the village and hospice exchanging hands on several occasions, only Locrehof Farm, to the south, was made as a lasting gain. To the north, towards Ypres, although the attack made little by way of territorial gain, it had a much more serious impact upon Allied thinking. This assault was made by *19 Reserve Infanterie Division*, *13 Reserve Infanterie Division* and *7 Infanterie Division* in the area between Vierstraat and the Bluff, on the far side of the Ypres-Comines Canal.

At the northern extremity of the attack, 2/39 Composite Battalion endured a torrid time. Reports of Germans massing for an assault did not reach brigade headquarters, whilst SOS rockets sent up to call for artillery help were apparently not seen in the fog. Promises of support had not come to anything, leaving an already thinly manned unit to do its best. When *393 Infanterie Regiment* came on to the attack, the composite unit was to all intents and purposes destroyed and German troops reached the Spoil Bank. One surrounded party, under command of Lieutenant Alexander Hall of the Gloucesters, held on near the canal until as late as 8pm, and at that point he and seventeen men managed to creep away to safety. Together with a party of about thirty men who held the Bluff on the far side of the canal, they represented all that was left of the battalion. Among those who lost their lives was its commanding officer, Lieutenant Colonel Hugh Robinson DSO, and Regimental Sergeant Major 200023 Bernard Stone DCM: of eleven other officers, it could only be said that one was known to have died and the others were missing. Of these, the second in command, Major Henry Howman, and one other had in fact been killed.

Although the German attack had been held, Plumer gave orders to take further action to reduce the Ypres Salient. Foch, imploring Haig that there should be no further withdrawal, made arrangements for more French divisions, artillery and aircraft to be moved to Flanders. He also began to suggest that the British should be relieved by French forces, which would therefore take over the whole front from Méteren, past Ypres to link up with the Belgians. The political and emotional weight of this suggestion for the British, who had been holding onto Ypres since 1914, with only a gap of a few months that winter, cannot be understated. In the event, it became unnecessary, for German intentions had, temporarily at least, moved elsewhere. There was still, though, energy for one last push.

The Scherpenberg.

At 10pm on 29 April 1918, von Lossberg telephoned through to von Kuhl, asking that *Fourth Army's* offensive in Flanders might be suspended. It had been a very disappointing day.

During the previous two days both sides had taken steps to reorganise their forces. There was no major action but shelling continued to be intense and there was a fierce local fight for Voormezele, in which 39

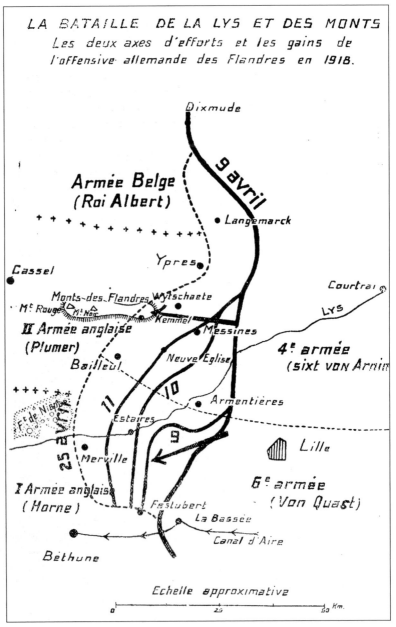

LA BATAILLE DE LA LYS ET DES MONTS
Les deux axes d'efforts et les gains de
l'offensive allemande des Flandres en 1918.

Dixmude

9 avril

Armée Belge
(Roi Albert)

Langemarck

Cassel

Ypres

Courtrai

Monts-des-Flandres   Wytschaete

M! Rouge   M! Noir   Kemmel   LYS

II Armée anglaise   Messines   4ᵉ armée
(Plumer)   (sixt von Arnin

Baîlleul   Neuve Eglise

10

Armentières

Fᵗ de Nie   11   Estaires

9   Lille

25 avril   Merville

I Armée anglaise   Festubert   6ᵉ armée
(Horne)   La Bassée   (Von Quast)

Canal d'Aire

Béthune

Echelle approximative

0   25   30 Km.

A simplified but curious French map, showing two axes of the German
offensive. A third, central, axis, not shown, was the most important of all –
the thrust towards the railway junctions at Hazebrouck.

126

Composite Brigade and later 89 Brigade (of the 30th Division) participated. Signs of another German attack were evident, with prisoners, deserters and air reports all suggesting a build-up and renewed assault. Allied artillery was ordered to carry out 'counter-preparation' fire on areas where German troops were likely to assemble: it appears to have been effective, particularly on the southern side of Kemmelberg, and a strong indicator to the Germans that they were unlikely to achieve any surprise when they attacked. By the time it took place, the French line was being held by 154DI and 39DI; the British, south to north, by 147, 148 and South African brigades as far as Ridge Wood, and then 89 and 110 brigades beyond, towards Ypres. In between the two *Entente* forces, 75 Brigade – which the reader may recall was the first to face the initial German attack near Ploegsteert on 10 April – was positioned, along with 105 and 106 Field Companies RE, half of the 6/South Wales Borderers and a company of 25th Machine Gun Battalion, to form a 'La Clytte Defence Force' that would be under French command.

Seven German divisions advanced to the attack at 5.40am, on a sixteen kilometres front from Dranoutre to Zillebeke, after gas shelling and what one British division described as exceptionally heavy, large calibre, high explosive shellfire. Many reports comment upon the intensity of German activity in the air, with one British battalion complaining that 'as many as thirty planes were over our lines at one time, and none of our fighting planes were to be seen'. The objective of the attack was to reach the line Ypres – Vlamertinghe – Reninghelst – Westoutre – Mont Rouge. It was not remotely achieved, although mistaken French reports during the morning that enemy troops had reached Mont Rouge were most disconcerting until the actual situation became clearer.

4 Bavarian Infanterie-Division and the *Alpine Corps* still held the left of the German front, and carried out the attack towards Locre, the Scherpenberg and La Clytte. The weight of their attack fell mainly on 39DI. Although a rapid advance was made, which reached Hyde Park, a position at the col between the Scherpenberg and Mont Rouge, the attack was badly affected by unexpected volumes of French artillery fire coming from the direction of Reninghelst. Machine gun and rifle fire also appears to have been more intense, steady and controlled than it had been four days previously.

The primary German gain near the Scherpenberg began with a rapid advance by the *Leib-Regiment* of the *Alpine Corps* around Fairy House and the Brulooze crossroads, in which two companies of the French 156RI were overwhelmed. Things had not been helped by the regiment carrying out an adjustment of its company positions during the night, which was only completed late and under the German bombardment. The strength of the German force had been whittled away by French fire, with many Germans losing their lives, particularly in front of Butterfly Farm and the railway line at Pompier. A German commentator would later describe the attack in vivid terms:

'The élan of the Jäger broke against a railway embankment, behind which French and English infantry were standing elbow to elbow. There, a real fire of annihilation decimated the Jäger. A hail of projectiles of all calibres fell on them without interruption and the number of losses assumed fantastic proportions. For its part, 31 Field Artillery was also very much tested. Of its thirty-six guns, there were only three left able to fire by the evening of 29 April.'

Despite these losses, the attack created a gap in the 156RI's line and the Germans pushed on. I have previously described the fighting here: it proved to be the very zenith of Operation Georgette in the Flemish Hills.

'The now familiar tactical doctrine was followed of detachments fanning out on both sides of the breach, wiping out the French detachments holding the front lines by attack from the rear from about 8am. The reserve sections of 6 Company fell back toward the Scherpenberg, joined by the reserve 5 Company and taking up a defensive position at the sunken crossroads some 600 yards north of Brulooze and east of Hyde Park. On their right, 9 Company in reserve, which had been in the small wood at La Couronne and holding another sunken crossroads behind it, suddenly found itself under attack. Within minutes the two sides were engaged in bayonet and hand to hand fighting in the wood, from which few Frenchmen escaped. The remnants of 9 Company withdrew north and gained touch with what was left of the rest of 156RI, now holding a south-facing line from 200 yards north of Fairy House across to 200 yards north east of Hyde Park, with the summit of the Scherpenberg just 300 yards or so behind. From this strong position it was able to pour machine gun fire on the attempts of Leib-Regiment to advance to Hyde Park and eventually found touch with 154 Regiment on Mont Rouge. Mown down by crossfire in these last yards of the slopes, the Germans could advance no more. On the right, parties pushed through Locre and Krabbenhof Farm toward Mont Rouge but a similar gradual gathering of French reserves and a number of

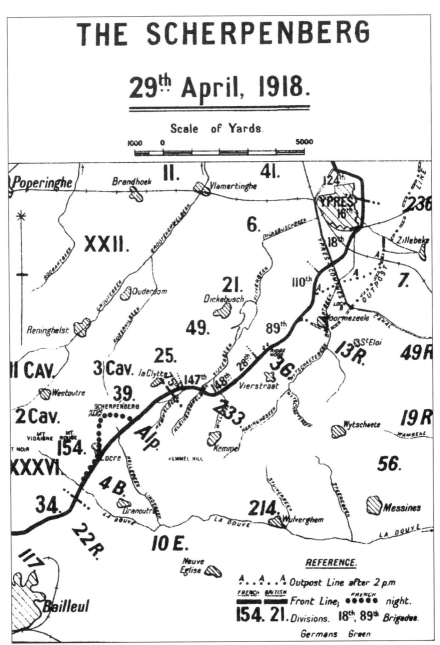

A map from the British Official History, showing the final, defeated, German attempt to capture the Scherpenberg. Note that the map contains an error: 28th should read South African.

localised counter attacks halted any further advance. During the afternoon, the French divisions mounted further attacks that drove the Alpine Corps back down the slopes and out of most of Locre. In the early hours of 30 April, the rest of the village and the hospice were secured.'

The 'La Clytte Defence Force' does not appear to have come under significant direct frontal attack; but it was obliged to manoeuvre to form a defensive flank on its right, to conform with the French being pushed rearwards. During the bombardment and while enemy troops were seen massing, the 8/Border's Lieutenant Colonel Charles Birt finally left the battlefield of the Lys at about 10am, having been wounded in the arm. Not long afterwards, his battalion's headquarters reported to divisional headquarters that, while no attack was coming in against them or the unit on their immediate left, they had seen the unusual sight, certainly by 1918, of the 7/Duke of Wellington's advancing with the bayonet to meet a massed German attack. The war diary of that unit calmly says, 'the brunt fell on D Company (Captain Conyers MC), who went out to meet him [i.e. them].'! Hugh Conyers was wounded during the action; one of an estimated hundred casualties sustained by the battalion. They had done enough, for, along with sustained volumes of fire from their trenches, no meaningful renewal of the attack was attempted.

Henri Joseph Saurat of 80RI saw service in Lorraine, on the Yser and at Verdun before being wounded by a shell at a position facing Kemmelberg in June 1918: a reminder that, while this battle may have officially ended, fighting continued in the area until the Allies launched their own offensive later in the year. (Europeana)

Not all actions were, perhaps, as dashing as D Company's bayonet charge, but elsewhere the units of the 49th (West Riding) Division held their ground on the Cheapside Line. Headquarters was able to report by 8.45am that the German attack against its line had been at every point repulsed, with exceptionally heavy casualties having been inflicted on the enemy, and that 'in spite of the heavy shelling our men are very cheerful over their success'.

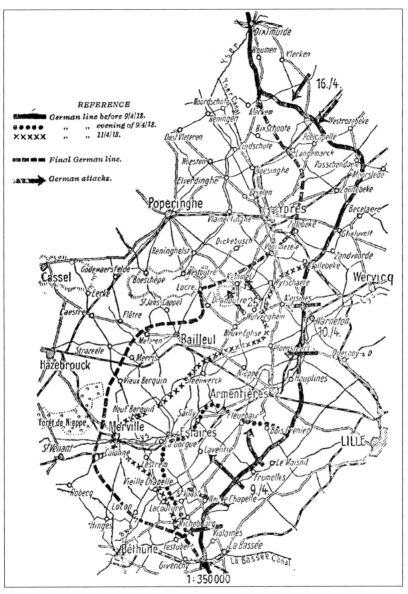

A map illustrating the progress of the battle.

'Georgette' abandoned.

With the realisation that its offensive capability in Flanders was now all but exhausted, *Fourth Army* cancelled plans for a renewed effort next day. The Ypres Salient and the line down to the Scherpenberg remained as active and dangerous as it had been since 1914, but no more major operations were considered for some time. A new offensive, Operation Hagen, was envisaged; but circumstances meant that it was never turned into reality. Flanders was not threatened by German intentions again until 1940.

But Germany as yet had considerable fighting resources upon which it could draw, and attention turned elsewhere. In a terrible irony, three of the British divisions that had suffered the most during 'Georgette': the 19th (Western), the 25th, the 50th (Northumbrian) – and, to a lesser extent, the 21st, were sent south to the Aisne in exchange for fresh French formations, and faced another onslaught on 27 May 1918.

Touring the Battlefield

By and large, the battlefield described in this book is a quiet, rural one today, although there are pockets of industry around Armentières and Warneton. It is also, especially in the area of the Flemish Hills, one of considerable natural beauty that attracts many walkers and holiday makers. In comparison with the southern area of the battle, covered by the *Objective Hazebrouck* volume in the Battleground Europe series, which is rather threadbare in terms of cemeteries and memorials of the battle, the northern area is remarkably full of them. Most, though, relate to different dates and battles of the First World War and as you travel the area you may find that you are distracted by the many sights that do not relate to April 1918. However, these do serve as useful reference points when exploring the battlefield.

Some general words of advice: first, the area is dotted with villages and small towns, many of which have good bakeries, small supermarkets and places where you might acquire refreshment. The larger towns all have petrol stations. There are few public toilets and you may wish to avail yourself of the facilities of a convenient café. In my experience, English is not widely spoken outside the towns when you are on the French side of the border; much more so on the Belgian side. Second, many of the places that are of interest are accessible via narrow, single-carriageway roads that often have drainage channels on both sides. These are not always obvious when the grass is grown, so take great care if you find you need to pass an oncoming tractor. It is important to be aware of the cycle lanes (which might not be altogether obvious) on bigger roads; you must not obstruct these when parking. Third, the local authorities in Belgian West Flanders have a maddening habit of digging up the very road on which you have carefully planned to travel. In many cases this is not signposted until the very last approach to it, and there is a tendency to dig across the whole road so it is impassable. Patience, some good maps and a keen eye for the diversion signs (*Wegomlegging*) will usually get you through! Finally, in parts of the battlefield, maize is a popular crop. Visitors in late summer and early autumn may find the cross-field views very restricted and I would advise you to go in the spring or early summer.

Tourists will find good information regarding accommodation and refreshment at the well-known websites such as Tripadvisor; but should also be aware that there are several Belgian and French tourist association websites and the very good 'Destination Coeur de Flandres' and 'Visit

Flanders' sites which cover this area. There are concentrations of hotels and restaurants in the larger towns, and many bed and breakfast and self-catering possibilities across the region. My favourites when staying here are in Bailleul, Godewaersvelde and Poperinge, but you may find the lure of the larger Ypres to be appealing.

Even if the tourist is equipped with the latest satellite navigation and GPS devices, they would be well advised to take some maps along for the trip. The best are those produced by the French Institut Géographique National (IGN). Their 1:25000 Série Bleue (Blue Series) maps are excellent for driving and walking. These maps can be obtained at many bookshops and even local stores and tabacs in France, and can be obtained from specialist travel stores in the United Kingdom. The Hazebrouck, Armentières and Steenvoorde maps cover much of the area of this book. The Belgian Nationaal Geografisch Instituut / Institut Géographique National produces similar series of maps at 1:20000 scale. The best for the relevant area is number 28 5-6 Heuvelland – Mesen. They also produce good tourist maps of the Ypres Salient area. Local bookshops, petrol stations and other outlets often stock these maps.

Tourists should be aware that Great War ammunition remains dangerous and it should not be touched. The use of metal detectors is prohibited.

Tour A

Breakthrough at Ploegsteert

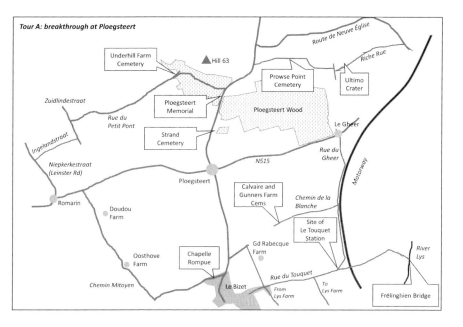

Tour A: breakthrough at Ploegsteert

This tour covers the area in which the 25th Division faced the initial German attack and covers the area of events which are described in the section 'Breakthrough at Ploegsteert'. We first loop around the area held by 75 Brigade, before going north to examine the actions of 7 Brigade. The length of time required for the tour depends on your own pace and the extent to which you wish to examine each site, but it is designed to be a full day tour.

The tour begins at the **Ploegsteert Memorial**, which is situated on the N365 Ypres to Armentières road, 1.3 kilometres north of the centre of Ploegsteert village and 12.5 kilometres south of Ypres. It is a convenient and historically important spot at which to meet and begin to take stock of the battlefield. Although there is some car parking space at the memorial, it is not a good place to leave vehicles for any length of time. Should you need to do that, you may find that parking at or near to the nearby **Plugstreet 14-18 Experience** site and which is described below is preferable. There is also a small car park at the *Auberge* on the opposite side of the road to the memorial, but this is meant for patrons.

The unusual memorial, unveiled in 1931, commemorates around 11,400 servicemen of the British and South African forces who died in this area during the First World War and who have no known grave. The deaths of the men who are listed range from October 1914 to late 1918; 5,300 of them lost their lives during the Battle of the Lys 1918. The River Douve, not far north of the memorial, is the official northern boundary as far as the inclusion of names is concerned; men who died north of it 'should' be listed at the distant Tyne Cot Memorial; but this cannot be taken as a rule that was always followed in practice. The missing men fought south of the Douve, through to the other side of Armentières and down as far as Neuve Chapelle, and west as far as the Forest of Nieppe. Beyond that, the men are listed on the Loos Memorial.

Among the Lys victims listed are three lieutenant colonels (Neill Campbell of the 8/Argyll & Sutherland Highlanders; Francis Studd of the Buffs, attached to command 22/Northumberland Fusiliers; and Charles Tilley of 18/Durham Light Infantry) and nine majors, many commanding their battalions when they were killed. The largest number of commemorated men are the junior officers, NCOs and rankers of front line and field artillery units, the bodies of many of whom fell into enemy hands as the Germans advanced. A considerable number of the names are of men who died while defending this very ground on 10 April 1918. But there are also those killed in some cases many miles behind the lines, such as two drivers of lorries of 604 Mechanical Transport Company of the Army Service Corps, who were far from the enemy and who were killed by very long range shell fire or bombing from the air.

The Last Post is sounded at the memorial at 7pm on the last Friday of each month, a relatively recent resurrection of a pre-World War II custom.

The Ploegsteert Memorial was built alongside the Berks Cemetery Extension, Plot I of which existed at the time of the battle. The cemetery was greatly increased in size when the local battlefields were cleared and particularly in 1930, when the nearby Rosenberg Chateau Military Cemetery and Extension was removed once it had been established that its ground could not be acquired in perpetuity (one of the very few plots that met this fate). None of the graves within the cemetery relate to the Battle of the Lys: the same is true of the small Hyde Park Corner (Royal Berks) Cemetery that lies across the road. Both are fascinating and you will find many notable and interesting burials, but if you are to complete this tour within a day we suggest that you return to them at a later date.

The magnificent Ploegsteert Memorial lists so many of those lost during the Battle of the Lys. (Author)

Before you move off, note the topographical situation. Across the road is the western edge of the dense mass of Ploegsteert Wood. The British front line lay about two kilometres away, beyond the wood and to the east, before the German attack began, and had been there since 1914. If you are looking in that direction, over to your left-rear is the slope of Hill 63, which gave a dominating view across the wood and to the valley of the River Douve to the north. It became the focus of much shellfire and fighting on 10 April 1918. The hill was, and is to this day, wooded on its southern slope: this is known as the Bois de la Hutte.

Should you wish to visit the **Plugstreet 14-18 Experience**, a small museum with good video and interactive media that provides context for those generally unfamiliar with the Great War, take the N365 in the southerly direction and then the first right, Rue de la Munque, and right again into its car park. The German advance through 75 Brigade took it across the main road in this vicinity and on towards Grand and Petit Munque Farms which are further on, beyond the museum. There is little to see, but you will note the relatively flat ground that was exposed to fire from Hill 63.

The museum's roof can be seen across the cemetery that is adjacent to the memorial. (Author)

Continuing south on the N365, you will soon reach **Strand Military Cemetery** on your left. Beware if crossing the road, for it can be very busy. Named after a communication trench that led from here towards the front line, the cemetery contains more than 1,100 graves; but only fifty-nine relate to the Battle of the Lys. Among them is Private 21525 Alfred Souls (IX. B. 9) of 11/Cheshires, who was killed on 20 April 1918 and was one of five brothers to lose their lives in the Great War. To add to his family's misery, newspapers had already mistakenly reported his death when he was wounded in 1916. Alfred was the fourth son to die: his twin brother was killed on the Somme five days later.

Three men of 6 Battery of 2 Brigade New Zealand RFA lie together in Plot IX, Row P. Their unit had been in action along both sides of the Ypres-Armentières road, just north of the Ploegsteert Memorial, when the enemy closed in on 10 April 1918. Another man from far across the sea is Private 7177 John Reid, of the 4th South African Infantry, which went into the counter attack at Messines. He was exhumed from the German cemetery at La Basse-Ville and reburied in IX. A. 2 in 1924. There is some mystery about the circumstances of his death, for German records show that he was taken prisoner on the Somme on 24 March 1918 and was in the administration of the PoW camp at Munster. Row A includes special memorials to five men of the German army who lost their lives during the battle and are believed to be buried in the cemetery.

Continue south on the N365 and enter Ploegsteert itself. On reaching the traffic roundabout, look briefly at the building on the right-hand corner. This is the old *Aux trois amis* estaminet, which existed before the war. Turn left at the roundabout, signposted for the A19-A25, and onto the N515 Route de Ploegsteert. The village is much expanded after its post-war reconstruction: in 1914 there were virtually no buildings along this stretch of road. Drive 2.3 kilometres, passing Lancashire Cottage Cemetery on your right and the mass of Ploegsteert Wood on your left. The whole area between the wood and stretching across to the River Lys, which is out of sight across fields on your right, was held by 75 Brigade; the next stages along the route are going to explore this area. Many of the trenches and farm buildings that can be seen today had been made into strong points and used by British forces since 1914. Ploegsteert Wood, nursery to many newly-arrived British and Dominion battalions over the years, can be walked (beware that the tracks become muddy and treacherous in winter) and contains several small cemeteries, dugouts and vestiges of trenches. You will soon come into Le Gheer, little more than a few buildings huddled around a crossroads, at which you should turn right onto *Rue du Gheer*.

It is unfortunate that the former battlefield through which we are about to drive has been sliced through by a motorway, which has not only led to a change of the layout of the lanes and tracks, but effectively cuts us off from the front line posts along the Lys, at least without making a significant detour.

Once you are clear of the houses of Le Gheer, the view opens up. You are now in the area held by 11/Cheshires. Their outpost line was across to our left, beyond the motorway which soon runs alongside us. The route takes us through the area of the reserve and support companies. Imagine this flat, rather featureless ground when it is in fog, thickened by the gas and smoke of shellfire: it takes little imagination to wonder how any direction could be kept, or to know what was happening. The first that the battalion knew that it was under infantry attack was when German troops were seen between our current position and Ploegsteert Wood, advancing towards Lancashire Cottage and Ploegsteert. This was mainly the result of 7 Brigade's front on the far side of the wood having broken.

Some 1200 metres from the turn you made in Le Gheer, a lane goes off to the right: *Chemin de la Blanche*. You can take a detour of a kilometre down this lane to two small military cemeteries, Calvaire

(Essex) and Gunners Farm, if you wish. The latter was the point at which the 8/Border met the 11/Cheshires. Neither cemetery contains graves of men of the Battle of the Lys, except for two Germans who are buried at Gunners Farm. They are principally of interest for their location and the preponderance of burials from the fighting of late 1914 and the first winter of the war.

Continue on Rue du Gheer, parallel to the motorway and you will reach a T-junction. Turn right. This takes you onto a narrow and in places cobbled lane, which is on the line of the old Armentières to Warneton railway. Within 200m you will find that you have entered an open square, used as a car park and bus stop. This is on the site of **Le Touquet Station** and a small railway siding there. At the far end of this square is the *Rue du Touquet*, and you will see a straight path or track, going off it at an angle and heading out into the fields beyond. This is also the bed of the old railway line, and in this case it heads away towards Lys Farm, which is on the river bank and was the extreme right of the 8/Border's front line. Several communication trenches and a light railway track began within the area covered by the square, going off towards the 11/Cheshires front line near Frélinghien. Just around the right turn onto the main road is Le Touquet Railway Crossing Cemetery, a plot of 1914 and 1915 graves that existed at the time of the battle. German infantry reached the area of the station as early as 5.30am in the fog of 10 April, threatening to cut off the companies of the two battalions that were still in the forward posts.

It is possible to make a detour to see the front line area and **Frélinghien Bridge**, from which German machine guns troubled 75 Brigade's front in the days preceding the attack. To do this, turn left onto *Rue du Touquet* and drive through the tunnel under the motorway. 500 metres past the tunnel, you will arrive at an area of open fields to your left and houses on your right. A track on your left runs down past a lone, small brick-built construction in the field. Stop for a moment: you are now on the British support line trenches. You will be able to see Ploegsteert Wood on the left horizon. The whole area within your view fell into German hands within hours on 10 April. Continue until you reach a fork junction and turn right for Frélinghien. This junction had been captured by the British in the Battle of Messines in 1917 and the area around it fortified into a small redoubt in the front line. The front line was some hundred metres along the right turn from the junction. The German front was on the other side of the river at this point, and you will soon approach the bridge over the Lys. For many years this was an international border crossing between Belgium and France, and the last building on the right was, and to some extent remains, a typical trading post, selling fuel, tobacco, chocolates and souvenirs. The current bridge was opened in 1961 after an earlier one, itself a rebuild, was destroyed in 1940. Frélinghien and Pont Rouge, further north, were vital crossing points for *214th Infanterie-Division* in the early stages of the offensive and their pioneers worked hard to create sufficient bridging across the river during the night preceding the attack.

Return to the site of Le Touquet Station and continue along *Rue du Touquet*, passing some factories and other industrial buildings, for about 400m. Take the left turn into a narrow lane, *Rue de la Howarderie*. It can be spotted by yellow tourist signs pointing towards a restaurant. This lane is often not in good condition, and in inclement weather can be very muddy and flooded. Take care. Follow it to the end, where it meets the River Lys, but, half way down, note where the lane does a small dog-leg: this is where the railway, coming up from Armentières, crossed the lane before it went on to Le Touquet. On the far side you will see the church spire of Houplines. Unlike Frélinghien, this lay in British hands and was in the area held by the 34th Division, for the front line crossed the river between the two villages, on your left. Turn right as you reach the river bank and follow the lane as it snakes around some farm buildings: they are on the site of a wired post that stood at the end of a long trench coming down from the main road, known as Railway Switch. More buildings soon appear on your right: this is **Lys Farm**, the right of the line held by the 8/Border. It was in this vicinity that German troops penetrated the battalion's line, soon advancing beyond it and also turning right to clear Railway Switch.

Continue to follow *Rue de la Howarderie* until you reach the junction with a more major road, the *Rue d'Houplines*. As you look left, you will see in the distance the Lys bridge crossing to Houplines – but turn right. It is not signposted, but you are now travelling towards Le Bizet. Drive for 1.4 kilometres through nondescript, flat farmland across which the Germans advanced from your right, until you reach a junction. This is **Motor Car Corner**. The road coming in from your right is the *Rue du Touquet*, which we left in order to see Lys Farm. You could detour here by taking a right turn to see Tancrez Farm Cemetery, which lies 550m down the road and on your left, but it now has no connection to the Battle of the Lys except for its location. Railway Switch trench ran up to the cemetery site from Lys Farm, and continued beyond it as Reserve Avenue up towards Ploegsteert Wood.

At Motor Car Corner, you will actually go straight on, but to do so you to need to turn left and then follow the road immediately round a small traffic roundabout, taking the first exit onto *Drève des Rabecques*. Very soon after leaving the roundabout, see Motor Car Corner Cemetery on your left. The plot existed at the time of the battle and was extended by the Germans; but their graves have been removed. With no other connection to the battle, note that the last graves in the cemetery are those of Australian units that were relieved from this area a few days before it began. They would soon return to Flanders, fighting in the area of the Forest of Nieppe. A light railway ran along *Drève des Rabecques* and there were several barbed wire barriers and enclosures around the two large and adjacent farms that lie along it: **Grand Rabecque** on your right and **Petit Rabecque**, closer to the road, on your left. Both had been used as command and communication posts but fell during the morning of 10 April as the Germans advanced through the 8/Border and 11/Cheshires, crossing your path from the Frélinghien and Le Gheer area on the right, pushing on towards Le Bizet on our left.

Turn left at the T-junction, onto the *Chemin de la Blanche* (the eastern end of which you passed after leaving Le Gheer). None of the housing and other buildings along this road existed in 1918: a sign that you are nearing the large, built-up area of greater Armentières. In 370m you reach another junction, this time with the road coming down from Ploegsteert village and heading into the border crossing town of Le Bizet. This is **Gasometer Corner**, which leading German troops reached by late morning, closing the pocket around the 8/Border, the remnants of which had to fight their way through this area to reach safety to the west. Sadly, the pre-1914 gasometer has long since disappeared, leaving this corner as a rather nondescript part of the battlefield.

Turn left (at the time of writing there is an Aldi supermarket on your left). After 200m and just before a petrol station on your left, take a rather unpromising-looking lane that leaves at an angle on the right. As you drive this short distance, you may found it hard to imagine that in 1914 it was a narrow, leafy country lane with, on the right, a wayside shrine, known as *Chapelle Mortelette* and dated 1645. No trace of it remains.

You have now turned onto *Rue de la Chapelle Rompue*, and in 300m will reach the ancient **Chapelle Rompue**. Parking can be difficult in the immediate vicinity but there are on-street places close by. It may not look it today, but this is an ancient and venerated site that originates to the first chapel, already built by 1343 and connected to the finding of a statue of the Virgin Mary in a willow tree. After its first destruction in 1566 it was derelict for a century and gained its current name, loosely meaning 'broken chapel'. Rebuilt or restored on several occasions since, significantly in 1898 and most recently in 1984, the chapel appears on all of the trench and battle maps of the Great War; but as far as I can ascertain did not have any military use and was by 1918 in ruins. It stood out as a valuable landmark, for example being used as the rallying place for the 75 'Brigade Group' of reserves that were to attempt to counter-attack towards Gasometer Corner and the two Rabecque Farms.

As the road continues past the chapel, it more or less follows the curving line of the River Lys as it flows past the north of Armentières, and passes through the villages of Clef de la Belgique and Clef de Hollande. The river is out of sight to the left. 1200m from Chapelle Rompue, and where there is an entry sign to the town of Nieppe, take the right turn into *Chemin Mitoyen*. For much of its length, this road is the border between France (on your left) and Belgium (right). After crossing the small Warnave stream, which is little more than a drainage ditch here, the name changes to the Flemish *Mitoyenstraat*. In the fields on your right the German advance came to an end on 10 April 1918: they had reached a position 4.3 kilometres from the original British front line at Le Touquet and had in effect broken 75 Brigade. You will see on your half-right in the distance the clear outline of Hill 63, which you saw at closer quarters when at the Ploegsteert Memorial. Drive 800m along this road and you will reach **Oosthove Farm**; another kilometre brings you to **Doudou Farm**. The line of the road was held during the night by a mixture of Royal Engineer companies, parts of the reserves of 75 Brigade and the 25th Division, and many British stragglers escaping death or captivity in the area through which we have already driven.

Continue to the end of *Mitoyenstraat* and reach the T-junction. Directly ahead you will see the higher ground on which Neuve Église stands. The German breakthrough in 7 Brigade's area north of Ploegsteert Wood helped it to advance towards that ground, which you will visit in another tour. Turn left. There are no signposts, but this takes us to **Romarin** and, if you continued beyond that place, to the main Armentières – Bailleul road at Pont d'Achelles.

The area through which you will now drive was crammed with camps and, mainly on our left, a major assembly of British heavy artillery batteries at Le Don. When the German renewed their attack on 11-12 April, much to and fro fighting took place in this area, with Romarin changing hands several times before the 25th Division was ordered to withdraw to a deeper position. Romarin, whose name translates as the herb Rosemary, has, like all of the villages of the area, been rebuilt; but its layout remains as it was in 1918.

We are going to follow the right-hand bend in the village at which point the road becomes *Niepkerkestraat*, but you may wish to take the short detour to Maple Leaf Cemetery. This is reached by turning left off the bend into Zakstraat and following it to bend right at the old Franco-Belge Estaminet. The cemetery is behind the estaminet on the right. It is another one that dates to before the Battle of the Lys. The cemetery was then used by German forces for nine burials of soldiers of *4th Bavarian Infanterie-Division* during the attack on Dranoutre and Kemmelberg in late April 1918. At the rear of the cemetery is a very good view across to Neuve Église and much of the area fought over in the period 11-14 April.

Return to the centre of Romarin and follow *Niepkerkestraat* beyond the buildings: Neuve Église begins to loom large to your front. You are on what was known to the British as Leinster Road. The 16/KRRC took up the line of this road and suffered severe casualties in their efforts to stop the German advance approaching the high ground that you see ahead. After 780m, turn right onto *Ingelandstraat*. This does not appear to be indicated by any signs, but is the first turn after leaving Romarin and is opposite a brick-built and rather pleasant farm building, whose roof tiles reveal that it was built in 1935. *Ingelandstraat* was known as Quarry Road. Hill 63 is ahead in the distance, with Ploegsteert Wood on its right.

Continue to the T-Junction with *Zuidlindestraat*, turn left and then first right onto *Rue du Petit Pont*. The German push reached the area of these two junctions on 12 April, as the breakthrough south of Ploegsteert Wood on 10 April was exploited and an advance towards Neuve Église was ordered.

After 2.1 kilometres you are in the lee of Hill 63 and reach **Underhill Farm Cemetery** on your left. This is another plot that had been in use by medical dressing stations nearby; it existed before the battle and was subsequently used by the Germans. Only one grave definitely relates to the Lys fighting: Company Sergeant Major 7139 John Smith, who was reburied in the cemetery in 1921, lies in Row D, Grave 22C. He lost his life while serving with 2/Worcestershire Regiment in the Neuve Église area on 12 April 1918, but the circumstances go unremarked in official documents and even the exhumation record does not make clear exactly where he was found. Smith, who was found below a wooden cross marked to 'four unknown British soldiers', was identified from his wristlet tag. When found, his feet were missing, and it may of course be that this was the cause of his death. The three other men, two of the Yorkshire Regiment and one of the King's Royal Rifle Corps, could not be identified. A Birmingham man who had enlisted in 1902, Smith had already had a short period as Acting Regimental Sergeant Major of his battalion.

Among the other notable graves in the cemetery (A.4) is that of Corporal 54571 Francis Vercoe of the Royal Garrison Artillery, who had already been twice awarded the Distinguished Conduct Medal, in 1915 and 1916. It is said that he was killed on 4 June 1917 whilst off duty and sitting reading outside his dugout.

Just 150m further on down *Rue du Petit Pont*, where the road bends to the right, is a house. This was built on the site of the former 'Red Lodge' which at times also acted as a dressing station and unit headquarters. Up on the slope behind it were a number of observation posts that had an excellent view across to Ploegsteert Wood and the area down to the village itself. There are vestiges of concrete remains here and there along the hillside, but for the most part they are well hidden and inaccessible. The Catacombs, a complex of tunnels and dugouts under the hill, may still exist and perhaps one day will be explored by battlefield archaeologists; but for today's tourist there is essentially no trace of them to be found. Contemporary descriptions suggest that the entrances were further along the road, near Hyde Park Corner, where *Rue du Petit Pont* meets the N365.

The tour now explores the area in which 7 Brigade fought against the initial attack by *31st Infanterie-Division*. The front line area is, unfortunately (and similarly to that of 75 Brigade), rather cut off and isolated by the N58 motorway; but there are some good points to see on the eastern side of that construction.

At Hyde Park Corner, turn left onto the main road (take care as this can be very busy, with high speed traffic). Directly in front of you as you turn is a face of Ploegsteert Wood, along which a lengthy duckboard track, Mud Lane, ran towards the front line trenches and posts some 3.5 kilometres away. The main road climbs steadily to breast a spur of Hill 63, giving good views across towards the wood. From the summit the ground begins to drop away gently to the valley of the River Douve. The river line was essentially the boundary between the British 25th and 19th (Western) Divisions.

Just over the summit, take the narrow lane that goes off to the right: *Chemin du Mont de la Hutte*. It is easily spotted thanks to a multiple green CWGC sign pointing the way to various cemeteries, and a yellow tourist sign indicating the route to 'Plaque Bairnsfather'. The area we are about to cross is much visited due to its connections with the Christmas Truce of 1914, and the plaque marks a cottage where the soldier-cartoonist Bruce Bairnsfather was located at the time. Interesting though they are, I suggest that you leave the 1914 spots for another time – for we have 1918 things to see.

After 650m the pleasantly-situated **Prowse Point Military Cemetery** is on your right. In use from October 1914 onwards, it fell into German hands on 11 April 1918 and now contains a number of German burials, mainly of men of *8. Rheinisches Infanterie-Regiment 70*. It is of interest that the German advance on the first day, 10 April, reached the fields that are just beyond the cemetery in the direction of travel. Across the road is the high ground of the village of Messines: its characteristic pepper-pot church tower is a valuable landmark. The Douve valley dips away and rises again in the middle ground.

Continue along *Chemin du Mont de la Hutte* and follow it around a sharp right-hand bend. The houses that you will now pass are the hamlet of St Yves (shown as St Yvon in some maps and histories). At 250m from the bend, on your left, is the site of the old Post Office, where Lieutenant Colonel Sholto Stuart Ogilvie of 1/Wiltshire had his battalion headquarters during the first hours of the battle.

At the end of the lane, turn right (into *Chemin de St Yvon*) and then immediately left into *Riche Rue*, which the army called Flattened Road. After 200m you will reach some trees on your left and a small electricity station on your right. Parking a car is not easy here as it is a narrow lane with few places to pull over. Do so with care, but you will probably only be here for a few minutes. In the trees is a large pond: this is the water-filled **Ultimo Crater**. Across on your right is a similar group of trees that surround the larger **Factory Farm Crater**. The two craters are the result of large underground mines exploded at 3.10am on 7 June 1917, the start of the Battle of Messines; they were the southernmost of the mines that were fired on that day. This location was, at that time, the German front line. The craters were also known as Trench 122 Left and Trench 122 Right, or Factory Farm 1 (Ultimo) and 2. After the British advanced across this ground and carried on in the direction of your travel, this area became an area of support lines where reserve units would be located. Ultimo Trench ran across the road next to and just beyond the crater. Ogilvie's reserve D Company of 1/Wilts was positioned here, and it was a place to which the remnants of his forward posts fell back after the initial attack.

Drive to the end of *Riche Rue*. Ahead in the distance you will see the tower of the church at Warneton, which is on the far side of the Lys and effectively the German front line up to 10 April 1918. The village of La Basse-Ville is in front of it on the near side of the river and was where the front line posts of 75 Brigade were situated. It would be possible by a long detour to see Warneton and La Basse-Ville; but I do not recommend it as part of this tour. Due to industrial development there is very little battlefield to see, although there are two New Zealand memorials in the area dating to their time here in 1917.

Instead, turn left onto *Route de Neuve Église*. The brigade's front line and the River Lys are across to your right, and you will now begin to see Messines and Kemmelberg in the distance ahead. Where the road begins a slight left-hand bend, you will also see a large white-painted building directly ahead. This is **La Potterie Farm**. You are now crossing out of the area held by the 1/Wilts and into that of 4/South Staffs. The remnants of their forward posts fell back from the Lys towards the farm before withdrawing further, going towards Hill 63.

Another 1.23 kilometres from the track that leads to the farm, and enjoying excellent observation across right to Messines, you reach another of the June 1917 sites: **Ash Crater**. This is on the left, also water-filled and with fewer trees around it than there are at Ultimo. Ogilvie's reserve companies were ordered to hold from this crater, across through Ultimo, to the edge of Ploegsteert Wood. You will see this in the distance and appreciate what a thinly-held line that would have been, manned as it was by just a few hundred men during the evening and night of 10-11 April 1918. The whole area around, and as far as the main road ahead, was riddled with trenches, dugouts and barbed wire defences.

Continue to the end of *Route de Neuve Eglise*, to meet the N365. A left turn will take you back past Hill 63 to the Ploegsteert Memorial.

Tour B

The Fight for the Messines Ridge

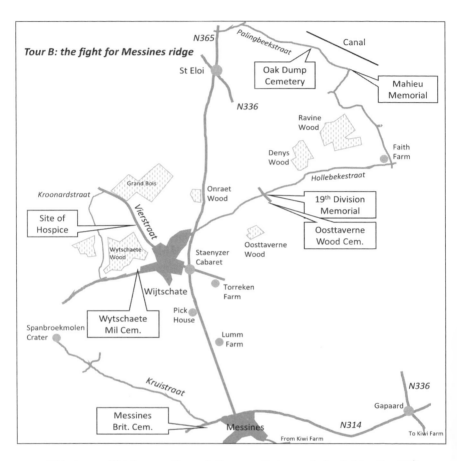

Tour B: the fight for Messines ridge

This tour will take you through the area that was defended by the 19th (Western) and 9th (Scottish) Divisions when the German attack began. It goes through the hard-fought areas of Wytschaete and Messines described in the chapters 'Attack on Messines Ridge' and 'Wytschaete lost, 16 April'. The length of time required for the tour depends on your own pace and the extent to which you wish to examine each site, but it is designed to be a full day tour.

The tour begins mainly for convenience although it does have an important connection with the latter stages of the battle, at **St. Eloi** (Flemish: Sint-Elooi), which lies on the main N365 road, 3.7 kilometres south of the Ypres ring road. The village is a crossroads on marginally higher ground than its surroundings, which condemned it to complete destruction during the Great War. It was fought over on numerous occasions and was a site where underground mine warfare was amongst its most intense. Heading south east from the central crossroads (now a traffic roundabout) is the N336, signposted for Armentières, Comines and Warneton (Komen and Waasten). Just 150m down this road you will see a tall electricity sub-station on your left. Park somewhere nearby. It is possible to find street parking places to leave a car in St. Eloi, should you wish to do so.

To the left of the tower is a lane, shown as a cul de sac, which leads to **Shelley Farm**. This is notable as it once again became a front line position to which British units withdrew in the final German attacks of the battle in late April 1918, with the line connecting up to Bus House which is on the western side of the village. Just behind the tower is a large water-filled crater, one of several around the village and the result of mine explosions at earlier dates in the war. The tower and crater are on the highest ground of the area, which was known as The Mound. From the lane on the right of the tower you will gain an appreciation that it does not take much to be 'higher ground' here. Two reserve companies of 5/Camerons were positioned here and held on under very heavy gas and high explosive shell fire when the Germans renewed their attack on 25 April; while their forward companies were holding the Dammstrasse, which we shall visit shortly.

Leave St Eloi in the direction of Ypres, drive 550m to turn right into Vaartstraat, which has green CWGC signposts to several cemeteries. Directly ahead of you are trees which are growing alongside the Ypres-Comines Canal; at the left hand end they cover the feature known as the Spoil Bank. This was man-made high ground resulting from the dumping of earth when the canal was constructed. Troops of *393 Infanterie-Regiment* reached that point on 26 April 1918, having destroyed in their path the improvised 2/39 Composite Battalion that had been holding the front line further to the right along the tree-lined canal.

As you approach the Spoil Bank, there is a lane that branches off to your right, named *Palingbeekstraat*: turn onto it and follow the lane until you reach **Oak Dump Cemetery**. Your route to the cemetery is through the area where 2/39 Composite had such a difficult time, being attacked in thick fog by overwhelming numbers of enemy troops advancing in our direction. The cemetery dates to before the Battle of the Lys but offers insight into what was happening here just before it began. In Row D are the graves of eight men of 180 Siege Battery of the Royal Garrison Artillery, killed together just a little further down the road on 28 March 1918 when a German shell exploded on the entrance to their dugout. They were only finally brought into the cemetery in 1927. The area of the cemetery and along the road was still occupied by such artillery units when the attack began on 10 April.

Stand at the right hand side of the cemetery and note the good view across to the spire of Wytschaete church. Beyond, on the horizon, Kemmelberg and Scherpenberg can be seen: this is the complete extent of the depth of the German advance during April 1918.

Continue driving along *Palingbeekstraat* and you will soon find yourself in the middle of a golf course. The development of this site has obliterated any trace of the Oak Trench, Oak Switch and Oak Support trench system that once ran through the area and which had been held by 11/Royal Scots at the start of the German attack. The road eventually takes a sharp right hand bend, at which find somewhere to pull off the road for a moment. There is a small stone **memorial to the Mathieu brothers** at the bend.

Auguste and Michel Mahieu were the only children of Auguste Mahieu and Marie-Louise Ferry, wealthy French textile industrialists and owners of an estate that extended across the communes of Voormezele and Hollebeke. In 1901 their existing house was demolished and in the same place an impressive chateau in white French natural stone was built, opened in 1905. It stood behind the memorial stone in the area of the golf course. The British knew it as the **White Chateau**. The memorial was moved to this spot in 2000, having originally been 400m further down, past the right hand bend, at the original entrance to the grounds. Auguste died at the start of the Battle of Verdun in February 1916, at the Bois des Caures; Michel was an airman, killed while serving with the *Des Chouettes* (The Owls) Squadron on 2 May 1918. There is a stone monument statue to commemorate the brothers outside a townhouse, also owned by the family, in Armentières.

Continue to the end of *Palingbeekstraat* and prepare to turn left onto *Eekhofstraat*. At the junction pause to take in the view. Directly ahead of you, a straight track (now gone) through a three metres deep cutting known as the *Dammstrasse* ran from the junction towards Wytschaete, the church spire of which you can see in the distance. This feature became part of the front line, once the 9th (Scottish) Division had reacted to the circumstances of the German attack and formed a flank to protect itself from attack from the area that was held by the 19th (Western) Division but which had quickly falling into enemy hands. It is a loss to battlefield tourists that scarcely a trace of the *Dammstrasse* can be found today except by observation from the air. Once into *Eekhofstraat*, the road bends a few times before emerging from the trees. Take the right hand turn onto *Duivenstraat*, at the junction of which is a small, modern wayside shrine. Just before you turn, look ahead and you will see the church at Hollebeke. We are now approaching the 9th (Scottish) Division's front line area. Delbske Farm, to which the line was pushed in the first hours of the attack, is down the lane that is now on your right as you make the turn.

As you drive down Duivenstraat, the land begins to noticeably dip in front of you. There are fine views on all sides: to your left is Hollebeke and beyond it on the horizon the Gheluvelt plateau of the Ypres Salient battlefield. Continue until you reach a crossroads, at the right hand corner of which is **Faith Farm**. On your left you will see Hope Farm, with Charity Farm just beyond it. The outpost line held by the 9th (Scottish) Division ran between the three. Ahead, the land continues to dip to the valley of the little Rozebeke stream, over which the *17th Reserve-Division* advanced through the fog. This was also the watercourse that helped Major Wilfred House of the Wiltshires find his way back towards British lines, further to the right towards Wytschaete.

Turn right at Faith Farm onto *Hollebekestraat* and as you travel note the mass of Ravine Wood and then, after a crossroads, Denys Wood on your right. With the Germans making great progress in the direction of travel against the 19th (Western) Division on the left, and soon reaching Wytschaete, the units of the 9th (Scottish) Division formed a defensive flank through these woods and held the line here until the renewed attacks in late April. The further you travel along this road the greater the sense of a gradual uphill slope towards the Wytschaete-Messines ridge, which now runs across our skyline. The last buildings on the left before we reach the main road junction ahead is **Goudezeune Farm**, which was part of 58 Brigade's reserve line.

The main road which you reach is the N366, coming down from St Eloi on your right. On the right of the junction is a house, on the site of what in 1914 was the *In de Sterkte Cabaret* estaminet.

On the left is the stone memorial cross **memorial to 19th (Western) Division**, in the same design as the division's memorial at La Boiselle on the Somme. The placing of the memorial is appropriate, for the division was also in action here during the Battle of Messines in 1917.

You may consider it worth a quick detour by turning left to see **Oosttaverne Wood Cemetery**, which lies on the right hand side of the road, just past the first houses. The original wood lay some way behind the cemetery, around the farm buildings that can be seen at about the same distance as the present-day wood that lies off a little to the left. It

The Oosttaverne memorial to the 19th (Western) Division. It is very similar to the division's memorial at La Boisselle on the Somme. (Author)

saw much fighting in 1917 and in the first two days of Battle of the Lys, as German troops pushed on towards Wytschaete, which can also be seen in the distance behind the cemetery. They recaptured some concrete bunkers, lost to the British during the Battle of Messines: two can be seen behind the cemetery today, in an area that was once a tangle of old trenches, wire defences and light railways. Many of the graves in the cemetery are of men whose remains were brought from far-off battlefields, mainly east of Ypres. Of the relatively few April 1918 graves here, some are of men who died of wounds after they had been taken as prisoners of war. An example is Leeds man Private 20186 Israel Sanofksi of 5/West Yorkshire Regiment (II. E. 10). He was exhumed with others from Hoogemotte Farm German Cemetery, east of Comines, in 1923. All of the documentary evidence suggests that he died on 29 April 1918. Another man to come into the cemetery at a late date is Private 32029 Samson Moulton of 2/Lincolns. He is a genuine Wytschaete casualty, who was killed on 14 April 1918 near Staenyzer Cabaret. Moulton was not discovered until 1926. Arrangements had been made to include his name among the thousands of missing men to be listed on the Tyne Cot Memorial, which was unveiled the following year. Two others were discovered with him, but could not be identified. They lie alongside

Moulton, whose grave is at VIII.B.14. Return to the *In de Sterkte Cabaret* junction and turn left.

Passing Somer Farm Cemetery, you approach the main road junction at Wytschaete. The tour will soon go into the centre of the village, but first turn left into N365 *Ieperstraat*, passing the petrol station on your right-hand side. After 500m of unremarkable post-war buildings, turn left onto *Houthemstraat*, signposted for Derry House Cemetery No. 2. The junction where you turn is marked on war time maps as **Staenyzer Cabaret**, after a building that was on the left-hand corner. The maps also describe *Houthemstraat* as dipping into a cutting, but there is no trace of this today – or indeed of the longer cutting that was on the village side of the main road, which saw much action in the various attacks and counter-attacks of 11-16 April. The Germans had built what amounted to a redoubt around the Staenyzer Cabaret junction, and it would come into good use in April 1918 when the British were in possession of Wytschaete and attempting to halt the German attack (which is, of course, coming towards you up the slope from the east).

Continue for 400m until you reach a large farm complex on your right. This is **Torreken Farm**, which formed part of the reserve 'Corps Line' of British defences that stretched up to and beyond Somer Farm. Behind it is the rather inaccessible Torreken Farm Cemetery Number 1, which was begun after the British captured this ground in 1917. Several German burials of April 1918 are there today. The cemetery area was reached by the long, duckboarded Dorset Track, which came from Wytschaete and the cutting. (The cemetery can be reached by returning to *Staenyzer Cabaret* corner, turning left onto the N365, then left again onto *Langebunderstraat*. A green CWGC sign next to a house 350m down this lane points to a lengthy grassed track to the cemetery.)

Turn to face the way you have come, and of course you will now have the German view. Across the fields on your right is the 'new' Oosttaverne Wood; the slight slope up to Wytschaete is evident before you; and the church of Messines can be seen to your left. Once back at *Staenyzer Cabaret* corner, go straight across the N365 and into the centre of Wytschaete. The village was completely razed during the Great War and all you see is post-war, much of it modern. There is a handy café on the town square, near to which is a memorial to the many men who worked as tunnellers in this area.

At the far end of the square, turn right and pass St. Menardus church on your right. You are now on *Vierstraat*. Continue along this road for 650m past the church, until you reach a sports centre on your left. Drive beyond it and park on your left, just past the farm on the right-hand side of the road. The sports centre is on the site of the large hospice – in fact an agricultural training school - that stood here in 1914 (it had only been opened in 1913). The building was completely destroyed by 1917 and the stark ruins became the subject of a drawing by artist Paul Nash. Behind it, Wytschaete Wood has regrown. Just past the farm, the view opens up to your right. A rough track goes off into the fields (which are private land) but peters out. The view takes in the area that saw most fighting once Wytschaete was in German hands. It is not particularly accessible, certainly by vehicle, and this spot provides the single best vantage point for seeing it. If you face east, looking into the fields, the wood on your left is Grand Bois. Moving around in a clockwise direction, there is then a gap before Onraet Wood. North House once stood in the lower ground to the right of the wood, but was not rebuilt after the war. This area saw several German attacks towards Grand Bois and the gap, and several counter-attacks as the British tried to wrest control of this ground and regain the heights of Wytschaete. It also saw a flare-up of fighting in late April; as one example, the 1/East Yorks suffered very severe losses at Onraet Wood. Behind you is Unnamed Wood and beyond that is the site of Black Cot, another battlefield landmark that was not rebuilt.

300m further along *Vierstraat* (you may choose to walk this historic stretch rather than move your vehicle again), come to a junction signposted for Croonaert Chapel Cemetery and Bayernwald to your right. The interest is, however, to the left, for the view now opens up on this side and the importance of possession of this ground becomes evident, for it provides wonderful observation across a wide area. Ahead of you, the road continues and eventually reaches the Vierstraat crossroads (at the large, light-coloured buildings). Just before you, on the left of the road, is a farm on the site of the former Red Chateau. On the horizon, right to left, is Scherpenberg, then the ridge that includes Mont Rouge and Mont Noir, then Kemmelberg. The group of trees that you see in the middle distance between you and Kemmelberg did not exist during the war, but on its left is Petit Bois.

Continue past the farm and turn left into *Kroonardstraat*. This was no more than a track during the Great War but cut through an area of trenches, dugouts and bunkers. The Wytschaete area still contains many concrete structures of both British and German construction, many within the woods, but you will spot others as you drive the area. Duckboard tracks and light railways crossed the lane as you reach Petit Bois, which is on the right hand side of the road. You will be on a downward slope at this point, on what was known as Vandamme Hill. In the fields on your right, just before the face of the wood, are two of the enormous, now water-filled, craters from June 1917. Passing the larger Wytschaete Wood

154

on your left, you will emerge onto the junction with *Wijtschatestraat*, which comes from Kemmel on your right and which was known as Suicide Road. Turn left to return to Wytschaete.

On the slope up to the village centre, you will pass **Wytschaete Military Cemetery** on your left. This was created after the war, and men buried here were brought in from a wide range of other locations. A splendid Celtic cross memorial to the 16th (Irish) Division is alongside: the division fought here in 1917. Only 330 of the 1100 graves in this cemetery are of identified men, and fifty-six of them relate to the Battle of the Lys. Among them are eight identified men of 2/Lincolns, with several others of the regiment who could not be identified with certainty. Seven of the men are from 15/Durham Light Infantry, which held the line not far from the hospice for several days and came under heavy attack on 17 April. Another six are of 4th Motor Machine Gun Battery of the Machine Gun Corps. Their unit had been in dismounted action up at Hallebast Corner and the Cheapside Line when they were killed on 29 April. All six were buried below a regimental cross, close to where they died, and were brought to Wytschaete in 1920. Another grave is notable for its scarcity: Corporal 2292 P. Eastwood of 4/South African Infantry is one of few men of his unit to have a known grave and be buried within the vicinity of his death. He was found mid-way between Wytschaete church and North House (II. C. 2).

Drive into Wytschaete, take the right-hand side of the square and exit onto *Staanijzerstraat* to take you back to Staenyzer Cabaret corner. Turn right on the N365 in the direction of Messines. The road closely follows the summit line of the ridge and gives good views on both sides. Recent building along the road can make identification of the various lanes and farms that appear on war-time maps rather difficult, but it is possible to identify some of the key locations.

In 560m you will reach an anonymous collection of houses, at which there is a bus stop on both sides of the road. This is the site of **Pick House**, which was on the right. Behind the houses (there are some gaps through which you can look, or possibly walk if careful not to damage crops) is where Captain Eric Dougall earned his Victoria Cross by bringing his guns to an exposed position on the ridge line.

In another 550m you will find a small lane on the right, called *Schoolstraat*. Opposite, on the left of the road and across a field, is **Lumm Farm**. The South African Brigade's counter attack coming from the right aimed to reach this point on its extreme left, and its objective line from there stretched ahead of you towards Messines. In another 100m or so along the main road, on the right, is the rebuilt **Four Huns Farm**, and soon after that on the left is the Celtic cross memorial to the London

155

Scottish, whose first action was here on Halloween in 1914. Soon after that, enter into the rebuilt and much-enlarged Messines and turn left at the first junction, taking the N314 in the direction of Komen and Waasten. It was known to the British as Huns Walk.

Continue for 2.5 kilometres until you reach the crossroads junction with the N336, which comes down on your left from Oosttaverne and passes through the hamlet of Gapaard. You are now approaching the front line area, held by the 19th (Western) Division before the attack. In the first hours the line was broken, and remnants of units were streaming back towards Lumm Farm and Messines. Turn right: this was called Hirondelle Road, and it takes you south eastwards towards the Rivers Douve and Lys and Warneton beyond them. You do not go quite that far, for the front line was on this side of the river. German troops came advancing towards you, having broken 7 Brigade's positions on the left of the area held by the 25th Division near Warneton, causing 57 Brigade of 19th Division serious problems. Hirondelle Road is now the *Chaussée d'Ypres*, for you have just crossed a cultural and linguistic boundary.

The front line posts were 700m along this road, in a flat and rather featureless area, although there had been a windmill on this spot before the war arrived here. The vista and muddy ground are not likely to lift anyone's spirits during winter. The two fronts crossed the road at ninety degrees but quickly bent round to the left: looking to your left, you will see red-roofed farm buildings 600m away across the fields. This, **Kiwi Farm** (or **Burghof** to the Germans), was behind the German front. This part of the line was attacked by *3 Hanseatisches Infanterie-Regiment Lübeck 162* of *17th Reserve-Division*, which initially advanced up the Hirondelle Road towards Gapaard, before turning left for Messines. Their assault fell principally on the 8/Gloucesters and 10/Worcesters.

Take the next turning on your right, the narrow lane *Chemin des Petit Bois*. It is signposted for local traffic only but is safe to use: take care in winter for, although it is a metalled road, it can be very muddy. As you go, you will see the tower of Warneton church on your left and Messines on your right front. After 460m you will pass a farm house on your left, at which point the road takes a slight right turn. From this point onwards, the River Douve is on your left, with the road getting further from it as you drive along. The river was the boundary between the 19th and 25th divisions. As the advance of the German *17th Reserve Division* made progress along this lane, flank defences were positioned on the river bank by its *226 Infanterie Regiment* to ensure no incursion by the 25th Division. The whole area between the farm and Messines was a mass of British communication trenches and dugouts, dating from when this area was captured in June 1917. Several key duckboard tracks, used for men, rations and material being moved to the front line and back, crossed the road at various points.

Continue to the end of the lane, at which point turn right to enter the centre of Messines. Like Wytschaete, it has been pleasantly rebuilt from utter destruction and has a number of shops, cafés and memorials that do not relate to the Battle of the Lys. It is worth seeing **Messines Ridge British Cemetery** and the nearby New Zealand Memorial. To do so, turn right on the N365 at the far end of the village square, then left onto the N314, *Mesenstraat*, signposted for Neuve Église (Nieuwkerke) and Wulverghem. The cemetery is easily found on the left-hand side.

There are more than 1,500 graves in this cemetery, of which just 579 are identified; and of those just forty relate to the battle. A quarter of them are men of the South African Brigade who went into the counter-attack north of Messines on 10 April 1918. As a good illustration of the wide area from which these men were brought into the cemetery, Private 241036 John Garfield of 4/South Staffs was killed on the same day but south of the Douve, in the area of Ploegsteert Wood and Hill 63. Garfield, a former chorister at Penn Church in Wolverhampton, lies in IV. D. 24. Another ten of the burials are men of the 12/Royal Scots, a battalion that was in effect destroyed in the area of Lagache Farm on 25 April 1918. These men represent fewer than ten percent of the men of the battalion who lost their lives on the day. The cemetery, a post-war development, stands on grounds that had been owned by the large Institution Royale convent, and the Cross of Sacrifice was where its windmill had stood in 1914. The 8/North Staffs advanced and held a line through this ground on 10 April 1918, losing more than 150 men while doing so.

The last leg of this tour is to **Spanbroekmolen**, another windmill site that became of great importance during the Great War and featured in fighting in 1914, 1917 and 1918. It is among the most-visited spots in this area because of the presence of the large 1917 crater, now known as the 'Pool of Peace'. But it is for its views that it is of most value in understanding the Battle of the Lys. To reach the crater, take the small *Kruisstraat* lane that heads away on the opposite side of the main road at Messines Ridge British Cemetery, and follow it across two crossroads, The crater is evident from the trees that surround it and a farm that lies nearby (behind which is a small cemetery).

Once you have found somewhere to park, and no doubt taken a look at the pool, walk around to the 'rear', east side, of the crater. You will be facing east. The rising ground to Wytschaete and Messines and the ridge between them is very clear. This was the obstacle facing British progress in 1917, and the Germans had fortified the spur of high ground on which you are now standing. The advantage of observation that the Germans

157

enjoyed once in possession of the ridge again in April 1918 is also clear, and you saw it for yourselves at Grand Bois earlier in this tour. Now walk around to the road side of the pool, for the breath-taking view ahead. In the middle ground on your left is the church of Wulverghem. Beyond that, on higher ground, is Neuve Église – and that was not only the Germans next objective once Spanbroekmolen was captured, but the subject of the next tour. From here, on a clear day, you can see far to the south, to the slag heaps of Loos and the heights of Vimy and Lorette.

If you wish to return to the start point at St. Eloi, continue along the lane; take the first major turn right for Wytschaete; and then left onto the N365, signposted for Ypres.

Tour C

Neuve Église and Bailleul

This tour covers the area described in the chapters 'Neuve Église' and 'Bailleul falls'. It is designed to be of about half a day in duration.

The Wulverghem-Lindenhoek Road Military Cemetery. (Author)

The tour begins at **Wulverghem-Lindenhoek Road Military Cemetery**, which lies 850m north west of Wulverghem. If travelling to it from that village, take the *Hooghofstraat* road that passes to the right of the *À la Basse Ville* café, signposted for Kemmel and Dranouter. It would be reasonably safe to leave a car here, if needed and with normal precautions, for there is on-street parking by houses opposite the cemetery. There is a good view towards Kemmelberg, along the road in the Lindenhoek direction.

Originally called Wulverghem Dressing Station Cemetery, a plot (now Plot I) of 162 graves existed at the time of the Armistice. The cemetery was greatly expanded to more than 1,100 burials through post-war

159

battlefield clearance, of which just forty-nine relate to the period of the Battle of the Lys. Of the burials, only 568 are of men who could be identified.

A special memorial in Row A of Plot I indicates that Captain Wilfrid Meir, whose death at Wytschaete was described earlier in the book, is buried somewhere here but the actual location of his grave is unknown.

Another noteworthy burial is that of Major Laurence Booth, 29, who commanded D Battery of 38th Brigade RFA. He was killed just north of Neuve Église on 13 April 1918 when a German shell made a direct hit on one of his battery's howitzers. An old boy of Winchester College and an accomplished cricket player, he had been in France since August 1914 and in the process

Major Laurence Booth commanded D/38th Brigade RFA and lost his life near Neuve Église. (Winchester College)

earned the Military Cross and Bar and was twice mentioned in despatches. His brother Francis had been reported wounded and missing while serving with the 2/Worcesters at Ypres on 25 September 1917. A joint memorial plaque in their honour is in St Peter's Church in Old Woking.

A unit with several of its casualties buried here is the Hallamshire Battalion, 4/York & Lancaster Regiment of 148th Brigade, which fought close by after withdrawing from the Ploegsteert area. It held part of the line during the defence of Neuve Église by the Worcestershire Regiment. The changed nature of the local Territorial battalions by 1918 can be judged by the fact that only one of the men commemorated here, Private 41968 Jack Blagbrough (IV.F.9), was actually from Yorkshire.

Leave the cemetery in a southerly direction, and on reaching Wulverghem turn right onto the N314, *Nieuwkerkestraat*. Just 170m from the junction you will cross the infant River Douve, which is only perhaps a metre wide here. Kemmelberg can be seen to your right, and the church at Neuve Église on its low ridge to your right-front. On your left, Hill 63 and Ploegsteert Wood are on the horizon. Just before you reach a gentle right-hand bend (about where the red triangular bend sign is located), an important light railway line ran across the road, linking terminus points at Kemmelberg and Bailleul across to forward positions north of Ploegsteert. After the bend, reach **Kandahar Farm Cemetery** on your left.

Although this dressing station cemetery mainly contains graves pre-dating and post-dating the time when this ground was occupied by the

Germans, it does include five burials from the Battle of the Lys. Four of them lie together in Plot II, Row H, Grave 26. They are men of 2/6th North Staffs who were killed on 15 April 1918 at Mont de Lille, near Bailleul. It appears that they were brought here and identified in 1923.

The grave of Second Lieutenant Anthony Johnson, aged 26 when he was killed (II.J.12), also appears to be the result of post-war searches and exhumations. The chapter 'Neuve Église' describes how he volunteered to break out of the besieged Neuve Église hospice to try to get a message to brigade headquarters, but was never seen again. One can only assume that he was found somewhere north of the village, for the paperwork appears to have been lost and no German or Red Cross records could be found, either.

As you drive closer to Neuve Église, the undulating ridge that includes Monts Rouge and Noir can be seen to the left of Kemmelberg. On entering the edge of the village, you will see a bus stop; a track going off into fields on the right; and, just after that, a left-hand road, *Zuidlindestraat*. Stop somewhere convenient. This spot was known as **La Trompe Cabaret** after an estaminet that stood on the corner. It formed part of an entrenched reserve line and, due to being on a height with good views to the east and south, was a key defensive location. It is worth taking a few steps along the roads in both directions, to appreciate the observation that this gave to the occupiers. The position initially taken up by the 2/Worcesters in the defence of Neuve Église is 250m away as the ground drops down *Zuidlindestraat* towards Petit-Pont. Its headquarters was set up in a dugout near to today's junction with *Bassevillestraat*, with the companies stretched across the road a little further down.

As German forces advanced on Neuve Église, the garrison of this spot, which at the time was separate from the village, found themselves being outflanked on both sides and the enemy getting around behind them on the Neuve Église side. The Worcesters made a gradual withdrawal, described earlier in the book, before an heroic counter-attack and 'last stand' in Neuve Eglise. Many acts of bravery in the lengthy defence of the La Trompe Cabaret junction probably go unremarked, but one stands out, not least because of what the officer concerned went on to do in his later life. In April 1918 he was the 32 year-old, promising artist Charles Sargeant Jagger, a Yorkshireman and a Gallipoli veteran. The History of the Worcestershire Regiment tells his story:

'On the left flank Lieut. C. S. Jagger wheeled the remnants of D Company to face the houses, held up the advancing enemy for some time and maintained his position until ammunition began to

161

run out. Then he withdrew his men by small parties from cover to cover to the buildings of La Trompe Cabaret. Scarcely fifty of his own men were still unwounded, but details of other regiments closed in on the Worcestershire detachment and Lieutenant Jagger organised the defence of the buildings with men of four or five different units. He held La Trompe Cabaret until reinforcements arrived: some platoons of the Hallamshire Battalion and of the 4/ King's Own Yorkshire Light Infantry. These were comparatively fresh, and it was arranged that they should take over the front line, while the exhausted soldiers of Lieutenant Jagger's detachment should be withdrawn to a supporting position behind a hedge some 200 yards in rear. There that last detachment of D Company lay down to rest. They were still under heavy fire, and presently Lieutenant Jagger was severely wounded and disabled. Lieut. Jagger was awarded the Military Cross. He survived the war to become a distinguished sculptor, the creator of the Royal Artillery Memorial at Hyde Park Corner [as well as the superb reliefs at the Cambrai Memorial].'

Drive into the middle of Neuve Église and find somewhere to park near the impressive church, *Onze-Lieve-Vrouwkerk*. You will explore the village on foot. The churchyard contains a small military cemetery, used by dressing stations based in the village throughout the war, with the exception of the period of its occupation by the Germans from 14 April to September 1918. It also came into use again in 1940. The village's own war memorial is at the western face of the church grounds, on the market square. The road coming up from the south that passes the memorial is *Niepkerkestraat*, known to the British as Leinster Road. Large German forces advanced towards Neuve Église up this road, having broken through the 16/KRRC's lines, and also up *Seulestraat*, which you shall see shortly. This spelled serious trouble for the defence of the village, for it meant that German troops had got in and behind the 2/Worcesters holding La Trompe Cabaret: the battalion was forced into a withdrawal, and moved its headquarters into a small brewery at the corner of *Niepkerkestraat.*

On 13 April 1918 an improvised but highly successful and bloody counter-attack took place, with much of the fighting being in the area around the church and market square. C Company of 2/Worcesters was by now positioned across Niepkerkestraat, about 200m south of the square; and 4/York & Lancaster and 4/KOYLI from the area of La Trompe Cabaret, having temporarily cleared enemy troops from the centre.

On the opposite side of the market square is a splendid, tall, Flemish-gabled building. As with all the others in the village, it was a post-war reconstruction, but essentially stands on the site of the original town hall. It appears that the functions of the building had been moved to the hospice.

Walk to the northern end of the square and turn left onto *Seulestraat*. In 190m you will reach a junction. The road to Dranoutre goes off to your right; *Seulestraat* continues ahead to Kortepyp and is one of the key routes by which German troops reached the village; another road goes off at an angle to your right. This takes the traveller to the high ground of Crucifix Corner and Ravelsberg, before going on to Bailleul. The junction was held by the Glasgow Highlanders, 9/Highland Light Infantry, but the enemy eventually pierced the gap between them and the Worcesters. The latter, now in real danger of being surrounded, moved into the hospice and conducted the famous 'last stand' action described earlier in the book. German machine gun units now established themselves at the junction and were able to fire up the Dranoutre road. Other guns were installed in the tower of the church, from which there was a clear line of sight to the hospice.

Walk 180m up the Dranoutre road until you reach the village fire station. Opposite, on the right, is the rebuilt hospice. It was renovated in 1999 and now houses the youth centre, *De Bosgeus*. On the front wall is an explanatory plaque to the action of the Worcesters in the hospice and in particular to the memory of Captain John Crowe and the act of

An informative plaque that is affixed to the front of the rebuilt hospice building, now called *De Bosgeus*. (Author)

163

extraordinary gallantry for which he was awarded the Victoria Cross. His escape from the hospice and his move onto higher ground can be traced to some extent today, although building work has changed the landscape somewhat. Crowe is said to have crawled along a ditch on the hospice side of the road, going uphill, and then crossed the road to get onto the higher ground which is now behind the fire station. Access is difficult but there is a gap before the last house on the bend, from which some of the ground can be seen. Major Laurence Booth RFA, whose grave you visited earlier in this tour, lost his life a little further around the bend. Alongside the hospice is a footpath. It pays to walk a little way along it for the good view across the village and to the Messines ridge beyond before returning to the centre of the village.

Leave Neuve Église by returning to the junction and taking the N331, signposted for Armentières and Bailleul. After leaving the built-up area it drops down through the area known as Trois Rois and passes the site of Kortepyp Cabaret. The sense of Neuve Église being on high ground is evident from the excellent views. The German advance towards the village largely took place on the left hand side, coming up from the breakthrough at Ploegsteert and Romarin.

At 1200m from the junction, turn right onto *Eikelstraat*, signposted for **Westhof Farm Cemetery**. Stop when you reach that location. The land in between the main road and the cemetery was crammed with several hutted camps, for until the German attack this was considered to be a relatively safe area. It is not easy to park as the lane is narrow, but there is a farm track alongside the cemetery onto which you may usually safely stop for a few minutes. The farm is the red-roofed building a little way down the slope, and the lane was known as Waterloo Road. The farm was used as a headquarters and dressing station, and the cemetery contains nine graves relating to the Battle of the Lys, all from its first day, 10 April. Three of them, all together in Plot I, Row E, were serving with 155th Siege Battery of the Royal Garrison Artillery, which was positioned west of Hill 63: it is known that Captain Walter Dyke was killed while taking ammunition up to the guns, and that Gunner 134637 Arthur Stroud died of gas poisoning. Two others in the cemetery are men of the New Zealand Field Artillery, which was also in action near Hill 63.

The view from the cemetery is excellent, particularly to the ridge of ground on the right hand side of the road, that runs from Crucifix Corner through the Ravelsberg. With Neuve Église falling into enemy hands, it became vitally important to hold this line, both to block the way to Bailleul and as a southern flank defence to Kemmelberg.

Leave the cemetery and continue along *Eikelstraat* for 310m, then turn right onto *Westhovestraat*. This will take you up onto the ridge. When

From Westhof Farm Cemetery, the ridge of high ground through Crucifix Corner and the Ravelsberg stretches away in front of the observer. (Author)

you reach the T-junction with *Heirweg*, turn left. Follow this road until you reach another T-junction, this time with *Kauwakkerstraat*, and turn left again. As you do so, look to your right for a good view of Kemmelberg and Neuve Église.

You are now entering the area in which the badly under-strength 59th (2nd North Midland) Division arrived during 14 April. This was stretched over a long line, from approximately where you have just turned, to Mont de Lille which is some 3.6 kilometres away. The division came under heavy attack next day by *117th Infanterie-Division*, *11th Bavarian-Division* and *32nd Infanterie-Division* with *11th Reserve-Division* in close support.

Drive 910m along *Kauwakkerstraat* and you will reach a junction with *Zwartemolenstraat*, which goes off to the right. On the left hand side of the junction is a crucifix, which gave this spot its name of **Crucifix Corner**. It is one of the summits of this undulating ridge road, and gives excellent views on both sides. 4/Lincolns of 177 Brigade held this ground, with 9/Norfolks just a little further along in the direction we have come. In that area were some trenches, some even with barbed wire defences, which had been erected some time previously as a reserve line of defence. The enemy attack came up the slope behind the crucifix (and through the huts of Vauxhall and Waterloo Camps) after a very heavy bombardment, and fighting was intense until the British line gave way on the left, in the area held by the Norfolks. Gradually, details of the 59th Division were forced to withdraw northwards; that is, down the slope towards Kemmelberg.

Continue for another 1.85km along *Kauwakkerstraat*. In so doing you

165

cross from Belgium into France and it becomes *Rue de Neuve Église*. As the road begins a gentle right hand bend, and the view opens up on the left, is the summit of the next significant peak: the **Ravelsberg**. Some contemporary and modern maps spell it as Ravensberg and both forms appear to have been in use, but British operational records invariably use Ravelsberg. At this point of the line, it was the 2/5th Lincolns of 177 Brigade holding the front. Their outposts were well down the slope on our left. The battalion lost over 350 officers and men in attempting to hold the enemy attack towards the summit and thence onwards to Bailleul. The views on a clear day from the Ravelsberg are exceptional, taking in all of the southern part of the Lys battlefield as far as the Forest of Nieppe. The characteristic tall pepper-pot shape of the church at Steenwerck is a good landmark.

As you continue to drive along the lane, the ground suddenly drops away and presents you with a fine view over Bailleul. The advantage that this gave to the German assault is all too clear. The ground soon flattens out; as you reach the edge of the built-up area, turn left onto *Vieux Chemin de Lille*. Just before the turn, a major light railway marshalling yard was in fields on the right of the road but there remains no trace of it today.

On reaching a crossroads, turn right onto *Rue Bellekindt*. The large and relatively flat expanse of ground on your right was the location of three British aerodromes, which were of course evacuated as the German advance approached. The modern Bailleul is much expanded, and the housing that you see on the right as you approach the town has sprawled over what in 1918 was open land. Park when you reach the large **Bailleul Communal Cemetery Extension**, easily spotted on the left.

The impressive and moving military cemetery at Bailleul. (Author)

This is one of the largest cemeteries in France, with more than 5,000 graves (if you also add the original military burials in the adjacent communal cemetery). Bailleul was the location of several Casualty Clearing Stations from the very start of the British occupation of this area, and the cemetery was mainly used for the burial of men who succumbed while in their care. It fell into German hands on 15 April and remained so until the town was recaptured in late August 1918. The cemetery was expanded somewhat after the war through the clearance of a number of smaller burial grounds. Just 103 of the graves are of men who died during the period of the Battle of the Lys, of whom thirty-eight are German. Most of the British died before Bailleul fell, and are for the most part in Plot III, rows F and G. They include three men of 208 Field Company RE, all killed when working to establish a line of posts between Mont de Lille and Crucifix Corner on 13 April 1918. The cemetery is mainly laid out in date sequence, and a walk along the rows is both educational and sobering.

Now drive into the centre of town. A one-way system near the cemetery forces you onto *Rue Paul Perrier* and thence to the junction with *Rue de Lille*, at which turn right. Bailleul is an attractive town but do not be fooled: everything you see is a post-1918 construction. Nonetheless, there are many architectural delights, notably in the many Flemish gable designs, giving it an air of the town's antiquity. Parking on the main market square is usually straightforward, putting you in the centre of the café and shopping highlights of the town. The splendid **town hall and belfry** will catch the eye at first, but walk down the short *Rue des Royarts* on its left hand side. You will then face the side of the church of St. Vaast which, when reconstructed, was unlike the town hall, built in a quite different Roman-Byzantine style to its destroyed predecessor. Facing the church is the town's **water fountain**, built in 1932 to replace the 1844 original. Its purpose was to alleviate the chronic water shortage affecting the town and it draws its waters from the springs of Mont Noir. Walk past the fountain and the rather unusual water tower, down *Rue du Collège*, to reach the **war memorial** on the right. The water tower was built on the site of a boys' school, one of the buildings that had been used as a Casualty Clearing Station.

The memorial retains part of the structure of the Church of St. Amand, which was destroyed in 1918. The same was true of a memorial to the men of Bailleul who had died in the Franco-Prussian war of 1870-1; when the new memorial was built these original names were not forgotten. The memorial also lists victims of the two World Wars, and the campaigns in Indo-China and Algeria.

Diagonally across the road from the memorial is *Rue du Maréchal*

Bailleul's unusual town war memorial. (Author)

Foch. Walk down it and turn right onto *Rue d'Occident*. In 140m, arrive at the **Memorial to the 25ᵗʰ Division**. This is situated in the middle of a busy traffic roundabout, so do take care when crossing for a close-up view. The division spent much time in this area, notably in 1917 and 1918, and the memorial includes a listing of its order of battle. The town was awarded the Croix de Guerre when the memorial was unveiled on 7 June 1921.

Walk back into the town square now but then take the left turn, just beyond the town hall, onto *Rue du Musée*. **Number 30** is one of the very few buildings to survive the destruction of 1918.

The final leg of this tour visits another area of high ground: **Hille**, towards which the shattered units that had fought at the Ravelsberg and Crucifix Corner withdrew, leaving Bailleul open to a direct advance.

Exit the town by driving to the town hall and taking the D23, signposted for Ypres and Poperinge. It becomes Route du Locre after a left-hand turn about 500m from the town hall. As you reach the outskirts of the town, pass the site of the former lunatic asylum (the 'Asylum' in so many memoirs of the war) on your right. This was used as a British medical centre from the October 1914 onwards, and is now an important centre for mental health. The gateway and main buildings have been rebuilt essentially as they were in 1914. Take the second right turning after passing the end of the very long wall surrounding the site, onto *Hillestraat*. There are no signs to tell you the name of the road.

Across to your right you will see the Ravelsberg ridge. You will soon find that the road starts to climb, and as you breast the summits of Mont Noir, Mont Rouge and Kemmelberg comes into view on your left and Bailleul behind your right shoulder. Continuing along Hillestraat will bring you to Dranoutre and the main road back to Neuve Église.

A Christmas card from the 25th Division, the British formation that faced the heaviest attack in the area covered by this book. (Europeana)

Tour D

Pont de Nieppe to Steenwerck Station

This short tour covers the German advance across the Lys at Armentières, up as far as Steenwerck Station. Central features to the battlefield here are the main Bailleul road and the railway to Hazebrouck, but yet another motorway now cuts through the area. Post-1945 building in Armentières and the Nieppe area has created an almost unbroken ribbon development along the road, obscuring much of the battlefield. It is also an area almost devoid of memorials, but the tour stops at a number of cemeteries, mainly for the tourist to get their bearings in relation to the history of the battle.

With the *Sixth Army* forcing a crossing of the Lys at Bac St. Maur, south west of Armentières, on 9 April and *Fourth Army* breaking through next day at Ploegsteert on the other side, it became inevitable that the town would need to be evacuated. The line of the railway and road became a corridor, along which the British fought a series of rearguard actions when forced to withdraw towards Bailleul. These operations were made more complex by the need to create a defensive flank on both sides of the corridor, lest the withdrawing force be cut off and surrounded.

A good starting point for the tour is on the north bank of the Lys, on the D933. There are two road bridges across the waterway, with the smaller and more north westerly of the two being across the original Lys. The larger bridge spans a post-war diversionary cut, by which barges can avoid a sharp and wasteful river loop. A large **memorial** stands on the left-hand side of the road, adjacent to the smaller bridge (if looking in the direction of Nieppe). A car dealership (Renault, at the time of writing) is almost opposite. It is possible to safely pull off the road on either side: beware, though, for this is a very busy stretch. The memorial commemorates an action in early September 1944, when Free French forces attempted to capture the nearby railway bridge to stop its destruction by the Germans. Severe fighting took place for two days, in which a total of thirty-eight Frenchmen lost their lives. Shortly afterwards, the Germans destroyed the road bridges and it is replacements that you see today. The bridges that were blown up were also replacements for those destroyed by the Royal Engineers once Armentières was evacuated on 10-11 April 1918.

The memorial is technically within the commune of Pont de Nieppe, which in 1918 was separated from Nieppe by about a kilometre of open ground. There was a similarly sized open field on the Armentières side of the river. The British had created a line of defensive posts on the Nieppe side, and units of the 34th Division moved into them as they began to evacuate. They were part of the reserve defences known as the 'Lys Line'. Burnley Post, the nearest, was situated just behind where the car dealership now stands. Manchester Post was behind the industrial buildings that stand behind the Free French memorial. They were both held by 23/Northumberland Fusiliers, who had been holding the front line east of Houplines and Nouvel Houplines before commencing the evacuation. They were forced out of this area just before noon on 11 April, as the Germans forced a crossing directly ahead.

Drive 850m away from the bridge and turn right onto *Rue du Cimetière*. In the 1918 version of Pont de Nieppe you had by now left the built-up area and were in the open ground before reaching Nieppe. This is, as you will appreciate, no longer the case. Drive to the end of this short lane and park near the gates to **Pont de Nieppe Communal Cemetery**. This is a fascinating cemetery that repays some time to study it. As you walk to the central crucifix, note that there is a British cemetery to your right and a separate German plot to your left. The British graves are of men who died while in the care of field ambulances and fighting units from October 1914 to March 1918, and again in September to November 1918. While the area was occupied by the Germans, they also buried in the same plot, but their graves were removed to the adjoining German cemetery in 1954. The British cemetery now contains 135 burials of the First World War and two from May 1940. Only three of the graves date from the Battle of the Lys, and are of men who died of wounds on 18 April, having been taken into enemy captivity. They lie together in III. A.1 and were alongside a group of German graves.

At the far end of the cemetery is the **Deutscher Soldatenfriedhof**, which contains 790 graves. It was begun in 1920 by the clearance of German graves from around the Nieppe area, but they were not permanently marked with the crosses and Jewish stele you now see until 1966. Three of the burials are of men who died in captivity in August 1914, but the others date to the Battle of the Lys and the period to September 1918 in which this ground was held by German forces.

Between the two military plots is the communal cemetery, in which you will find many graves with the red, white and blue *Souvenir Francis* symbol, marking the last resting place of a First World War soldier and of many who died with the Free French forces in the Second World War. The Nieppe area appears to have been one where subversive activities became intensive after the Fall of France.

Return to the main road and turn right towards Nieppe. You very soon approach a traffic roundabout, which is on the site of part of another reserve line of trenches, the 'Nieppe Line'. Continue to enter Nieppe and then turn left at the traffic roundabout, which is just past the large Église St. Martin. You are now on the *Rue du Dr Henri Vanuxeem*, named after the mayor of Nieppe from 1906 to 1939. This road eventually crosses the railway at Touquet Parmentier, where Nieppe Station stood during the Great War.

300m after the railway, turn right at the junction into *Rue du Bas Chemin*. Along this road, the battalions of 101st Brigade were deployed to hold a flank defence as far north as Trois Arbres, from where it was carried on by 88th Brigade to Steenwerck Station. This defence was to ensure the safety of the units that withdrew from Pont de Nieppe and Nieppe during the night of 11 April.

The road eventually runs parallel to the railway. Turn right at the first opportunity, to cross the railway at Kellow Crossing. This puts you onto *Rue des Trois Arbres*, which goes through the hamlet of Le Veau. During the night 9-10 April 1918, a counter-attack by cooks, transport men and other details of the 34th Division, drove back an enemy incursion back to the crossing. On reaching the T-junction with the D77 *Rue des Meuniers*, turn left. Shortly after re-crossing the railway, arrive at **Trois Arbres Cemetery** on the right.

The cemetery resulted from the positioning of a Casualty Clearing Station here from 1916, but it was greatly enlarged by battlefield clearance after the war and now contains 1,704 graves. One of the results of this is that Trois Arbres contains a significant number of graves of men who died in 1914 and 1915. The ground occupied by the cemetery as it was at the time of the battle was captured by the Germans on 11 April 1918, held up for a day by the 34th Division's flank defence, holding off a German advance coming from Steenwerck. There are ninety-seven graves of men who died during the Battle of the Lys, but virtually all were brought into the cemetery's Plots II and III after the war. The course of the battle is well represented here: 8/Border from Ploegsteert in the first days; 6 and 7/Duke of Wellington's at Nieppe; 11/Lancashire Fusiliers, just down the road at Steenwerck. Five officers and men of the Royal Guernsey Light Infantry are also here, killed in the fighting near Doulieu.

Continue along *Rue des Meuniers* and cross the motorway. Turn left as the road descends from the bridge, signposted for **Deutsche Soldatenfriedhof Steenwerck**. Now the resting place of 2,048 German soldiers, the majority dating from the Battle of the Lys and in the period when the Allied counter-offensive recaptured this ground, the cemetery was not permanently finished until 1979. The last twelve graves were dug in 1969, when remains were found during construction work.

Returning to the main road, turn left and enter Steenwerck. Note a particularly fine Flemish-style 'Bruges Gothic' house on the right. The town was taken by the Germans on 10 April and suffered almost total devastation. You may enjoy a quick detour into the pleasantly rebuilt town centre to see the church, completed in 1928, and the unusual **war memorial** that stands facing it. This will require you to make a left turn, signposted for Centre Ville, but note a right turn that is just beyond it: after the detour, you leave Steenwerck by this right turn, which is the N38 *Rue de la Gare*.

The road takes a left hand bend to cross the motorway, but you will see the line of the old road ahead as you turn. In 650m from the motorway bridge, reach **Steenwerck Station**, around which a small village of sorts had grown even before 1914. The station was a key point in the flank defence. Note that once over the railway there are good views towards the Flemish Hills.

Continue along the D38 until the junction is reached with the D933 *Route de Lille* at De Seule (or Le Seau, for this appears to be right on the linguistic boundary). Turn right for Nieppe. Very soon afterwards you will see on the left the start of the Kortepyp road, which rises to Neuve Église. Carrying straight on, in 1300m turn left onto Rue du Sac. **Pont d'Achelles Military Cemetery** is on the right.

A burial plot that existed before the Royal Newfoundland Regiment and 2/Monmouths fought to defend Pont d'Achelles on 11 April 1918, it now also contains German graves from the time they held this ground. Private 265888 Arthur Baggs of the Monmouths appears to have died of wounds, having recently been taken prisoner, but he was not brought into the cemetery until 1922 (III. A. 20). German records confirm that he was at first buried near to the main road. Not far from Baggs is the grave of Major Joseph Husband (II. G. 2) of C Company, 59th Machine Gun Battalion. An educated man with an MA in English and History, he had twice been mentioned in despatches. With a lieutenant and a detachment of ten men, on 11 April he had tried to recapture a farm near Papot, from which the enemy's machine guns were proving

Major Joseph Husband MA of 59th Machine Gun Battalion died in a counter-attack near Papot. (Author)

troublesome. He sustained a bullet wound to the chest and died at the dressing station that was at that time still alongside the cemetery.

Return to the main road and turn left. 350m further on, you will see a gated lane on your right. This is private access to the site of **Papot Mill,** where five brigadier generals met to confer on 11 April 1918. Continue along the road to return to Nieppe.

Tour E

Kemmelberg and the Flemish Hills

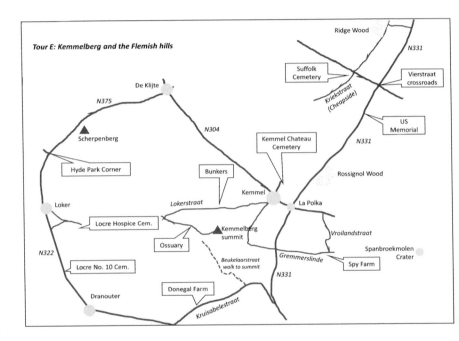

Tour E: Kemmelberg and the Flemish hills

For convenience and as a landmark, this tour begins at the **Vierstraat crossroads** on the N331 Ypres to Kemmel road. It is easily identified by the huge prefabricated concrete buildings of the Goudezeune Prefab Company. It is a pity that the buildings mask what was once an excellent 360-degree view from the crossroads, but a short walk in the Kemmel direction soon opens it up. The ground slopes gently away on the left before rising again to Messines Ridge. The several woods in front of Wytschaete can clearly be seen, as can the spires of the churches of both villages. The German attack had secured the ridge and captured Wytschaete and the woods by 16 April, but drove through Vierstraat on 25-26 April and reached the British defences of the Cheapside Line.

Ahead, down the road and slightly across on our right, Kemmelberg is the nearest and most dominant feature, but the range of the other Flemish Hills can also be seen. A short walk the other way, towards Ypres, soon gives the impression of Vierstraat being at the top of a gentle spur of higher ground that stretches from Kemmelberg. An ideally situated tower windmill had stood near the crossroads before the war.

Take the road, also called *Vierstraat*, that runs northwards through the prefab factory buildings, and after 520m turn left onto *Kriekstraat*. You are now on the position of the Cheapside Line, beyond which German forces did not progress. Just before the turn, see a **demarcation stone** on the left hand side of the road. It is one of 119 that were located by the Touring Club de France and the Touring Club de Belgique to mark the deepest penetration by the Germans, and is marked 'Here the invader was brought to a standstill'. This one is topped by a French helmet. This stone has been moved on several occasions and the helmet does not reflect the fact that it was the British 49th (West Riding) Division that held the Cheapside Line here.

Just a few metres after the turn, you will see **Suffolk Cemetery** on the right. There is a place to pull over and park. Originally known as Cheapside Cemetery, it contains only forty-seven graves, of which twenty are men of 4/ and 5/York & Lancaster Regiment who died defending this position in April 1918. They were brought in by 38 Labour Group in October 1918, after the Allied counter-attack had pushed the enemy away, joining original burials of the 2/Suffolks from 1914 and 1915. Another small cemetery, but with less direct connection to the battle, lies further along the lane, at Godezonne Farm. Return to the junction and continue across the small dog-leg.

Note that you could turn left for a short detour to see the much larger **Klein-Vierstraat British Cemetery**. This was begun in January 1917 and used by field ambulances and fighting units before the middle of January 1918. Plot IV was begun in April 1918. After the Armistice, graves were brought into Plots I and IV to VII from two smaller cemeteries and from the battlefield areas of Dickebusch, Locre and Kemmel. The cemetery now contains 805 First World War burials, 109 of them remaining unidentified. My attention was taken by the grave of Private 41567 George Robertson, a lad from Penicuik, typical of the 18 year-old 'A4' conscripted men hurriedly sent overseas during the crisis. He lies in IV. G 3. Robertson was enlisted in January 1917, was sent to France on 2 April and posted to join 2/Royal Scots Fusiliers ten days later. He was killed in the final fighting near Ridge Wood on 29 April and originally buried there, being brought into the cemetery in late 1919. His is one of the youngest of the 103 burials from the period of the Battle of the Lys. If you undertook this detour, return to the junction and turn left.

Continue for a kilometre, with the large **Ridge Wood** being on your left for the final few hundred metres. The German advance in late April reached the wood but was halted there, although some parts of it remained contested until the enemy was finally ejected in July 1918. A left turn into the wood would take you to the large Ridge Wood Military Cemetery but, of the more than 600 graves dating from 1915 onwards, only three relate to April 1918, presumably as it was now too close to the front line trenches to be considered practical for burials. A number of French graves of the battle have been removed to other burial grounds.

A right turn facing the wood, onto *Slijpstraat*, takes you back towards the main Ypres-Kemmel road. You pass at the junction Elzenwalle Brasserie Cemetery, named after a brewery that stood across the road. This entirely dates to 1917 and earlier, and was fought over in late April 1918. A long duckboard track, going off towards St Eloi, followed the line of *Slijpstraat*.

Turn right, and soon pass across Vierstraat crossroads again. Enjoy the excellent views on both sides of this ridge road, and note the **monument to the United States 27th and 30th Divisions**, who took part in offensive operations here later in 1918, on your left. The demarcation stone that you saw near Vierstraat stood alongside this monument for many years: a completely inappropriate and misleading choice.

After 1300m from Vierstraat, reach **La Laiterie Military Cemetery** on the right. This existed during the battle and fell into German hands. It was greatly expanded after the Armistice and now contains more than 750 graves, but only nine are of April 1918.

As you continue in the Kemmel direction, you see a mass of trees on the left. This is **Rossignol Wood**, a place where British troops were sheltered and assembled as reserves until it was captured in the German attack on Kemmelberg on 25 April. Their advance took them some kilometre across to the right, reaching Beaver Corner and the end of the Cheapside Line, now the right-hand end of the British-held sector, with French troops beyond.

You will soon reach a traffic roundabout: the junction known as **La Polka** and named after 'La Grande Polka Cabaret', which stood on the left, just before the roundabout, in 1914. Turn left, onto *Wijtschatestraat*.

610m from the roundabout you will reach a right-hand turn into *Vroilandstraat*. Follow this road through a few bends, as the ground rises before you, until you arrive at a junction. Ahead of you is **Spy Farm**, which sits at the end of a flattish spur of ground coming from Kemmelberg. This high ground – known as the 'Lindenhoek – Vroilandhoek plateau' – was recognised by both sides as being important to the secure occupation of Kemmelberg, which is now very evident on your right. German plans allowed for the attack on the ground to proceed fifteen minutes earlier than the rest of its assault on 25 April, to ensure

Kemmelberg and the Flemish Hills are once again important and well visited spots on the tourist trail. This view is from the Neuve Église to Dranoutre road. (Genevra Charsley)

that French troops could not pour fire from the Spy Farm area down the slopes that surround it.

Turn right just before the farm, onto *Gremmerslinde*, and follow it to the junction with the N331 *Kemmelstraat* at Lindenhoek. You are still on the plateau, but the ground is now visibly rising towards Kemmelberg. By April 1918 this area was a mass of hutted camps and was also entrenched as part of a reserve line coming from Neuve Église. Continue across the junction and in a short distance pass by Lindenhoek Chalet Military Cemetery on the right. This is another burial plot that existed at the time of the battle and which was greatly expanded after the war. Nine men who died in April 1918 lie here, all in Plot II, but from a variety of units and apparently all brought in from elsewhere.

You are now going to take a look at Kemmel village before you return to the hill itself. Continue for 200m past the cemetery and turn right onto *Kattekerkhofstraat*, soon passing the 'De Lork' youth centre on the left. Emerge and turn right onto *Bergstraat*. A drive of 600m brings you into the green village square, complete with bandstand and looking very much as it did in 1914: except that, like other places we have seen, it was entirely rebuilt after the war. Turn left towards the church of St. Laurentius and follow the road through the church gates. The **churchyard** contains twenty-five most interesting military burials from 1914 and 1915, including Second Lieutenant Frederick Turner of the Liverpool Scottish, who died on 10 January 1915. Some CWGC documentation suggests that he and the others were considered for removal to Wulverghem-Lindenhoek Road Military Cemetery in 1919 but this was for some reason not followed through. Turner was the current Captain of the Scotland rugby XV and also an accomplished cricketer.

Near to the church is the **Toerisme Heuvelland Visitors Centre**. This is not only the best place for information regarding accommodation and things to see and do in the area, but also runs very good Great War exhibitions.

Return to the village square and follow the road out to your left. You will soon reach a T-junction at which you will turn left onto *Reninghelstraat*, but first look to your right. The trees that you can see are part of a large area of land that once included Kemmel Chateau and stretched for a considerable distance behind the buildings that are in front of you.

Take the first right, *Nieuwstraat*, and follow it for 325m to reach **Kemmel Chateau Military Cemetery**. This is an impressive and pretty plot of more than 1,100 graves, with many a story to tell – but not a single one dates to the Battle of the Lys. Walk a few steps beyond the cemetery and the new communal cemetery next to it, to gain a good view. Across to your right is Rossignol Wood, which you passed when on the road to La Polka. The trees closer to you and behind the cemetery were part of the chateau estate. Out of sight on our left, due to buildings, is the little Kemmelbeek or Vijverbeek, the rapid and unexpected flooding of which badly disrupted British and French attempts to recapture Kemmel after its initial capture on 25 April.

Return to *Reninghelstraat*, turn right and follow it out of Kemmel, past the old chateau site, to La Polka. Turn right at the traffic roundabout and follow the long slope up to the plateau crossroads at Lindenhoek.

Kemmel was another village that suffered almost total devastation during the battle. (Author)

Carry straight on and the road begins to dip on the other side of the plateau; the view across to Kemmelberg on your right and to the Dranoutre and Locre areas just to the left of it opens up. In 950m from Lindenhoek, turn right onto *Kruisabelestraat*, signposted for Dranoutre.

After a drive of 720m from the turn, the last part of which is past a long, left hand bank, you will see a picnic table and the start of a marked walking path on the right. This is one of several such paths that go in the general direction of Kemmelberg, and they can be extraordinarily busy at weekend and on fine days: beware the possibility of distracted pedestrians and cyclists in this area. A few metres ahead is *Beukelaarstraat*, which is a metaled road and can be driven, but which is essentially also a tourist route. I can make no greater recommendation than you leave the car for a while and walk up and down this route, even if only part way to the top of the hill, for you will gain no better education about the task confronting both attackers and defenders. If you plan to walk for any distance, take the wise precautions of having plenty of water with you and either remove valuables from your vehicle or make sure they are secure and out of sight. Part-way up, take the right fork just after the small chapel, then carry on in a straight line. The path takes you all the way to the summit. As you begin the walk, you are in the French front line posts, and soon climb to their support positions. Turn around to look back towards the Germans: you will appreciate that you are completely exposed to their view. This area was pulverised by the bombardment that preceded the battle, and in retrospect it is clear that the French deployed too many men in these positions, leaving too few behind the hill to be called upon for counter-attack purposes. Continue walking and your legs and back will likely begin to remind you of the sheer physical demand on the *Alpine Corps*, fighting their way behind a creeping barrage through devastated ground, up the ever-steepening sides. You will be returning to the sites at the summit, so do not worry if your legs or energy are flagging!

Back down where *Beukelaarstraat* begins, just ahead of you, up the slope and on the right of the road, is **Aircraft Farm**. Along with **Donegal Farm,** which you shall soon reach and is the second large farm on the right, this formed part of the French front line protecting Kemmelberg. The *Alpine Corps* assembled in the fields of your left, ready to make the assault against them. Continue along *Kruisabelestraat* until you reach Dranoutre, noting how Kemmelberg looks much more shallow and less threatening from this direction.

Both Dranoutre and nearby Locre had been in use for billeting British units since late 1914 and consequently many camps existed nearby. Medical facilities, stores, estaminets and more made them both far much more lively than the once-again small, sleepy, pretty places that are now. There are early war burials in both churchyards, and larger military cemeteries that existed in April 1918 but were later expanded. You can largely pass them by for the purposes of this tour, for their Battle of the Lys casualties are almost zero. Dranoutre was captured by the Germans on 25 April 1918 after they overcame 154DI.

Follow the road bend near the church in Dranoutre to go towards Locre, and as soon as you leave the village a whole new vista becomes apparent. Kemmelberg is on our right, but to the half-right is the characteristic, half-wooded hump of Scherpenberg. The German offensive was finally brought to a halt there on 29 April.

You eventually reach the unusual, open-fronted and beautifully situated **Locre Number 10 Cemetery**. This was begun by French units during the intensive, to and fro, fight for Locre once Dranoutre had fallen. The graves of 248 French soldiers were later removed to another burial ground, and British and German graves were brought into the cemetery from the battlefields after the Armistice. They all date to later fighting as the Allies began a counter-offensive here, so you have the unusual scenario of a wholly Battle of the Lys cemetery now containing none of the dead of the battle. The views from the cemetery make a stop worthwhile. Nearest to you, to the left and on the other side of the road, is Locrehof Farm, which was captured by *4th Bavarian Infanterie-Division* on 26 April.

Continue 800m towards Locre and turn right into *Dondeyneweg*. You will soon pass on your left a large building, the rebuilt Convent of St. Antoine, which was also known as the Hospice. This building, which essentially stood alone during the war, as Locre was very much smaller than it is now, was used by British field ambulances. By the end of April 1918 it was completely destroyed, having been a point of considerable fighting during the French defence of this ground in 27-30 April. Inevitably a military cemetery had grown alongside the hospice. Follow the road as it passes the hospice and becomes *Godtschalkstraat* for another 285m and you will see on the right a grassed path to **Locre Hospice Cemetery**. It attracts more than the usual share of battlefield tourists, possibly mainly because of the adjacent presence of the isolated grave of Irish nationalist politician and MP for Wexford, Major William Redmond, of 6/Royal Irish Regiment.

The cemetery contains the graves of thirty-two British and two German officers and men who lose their lives during the battle. They include the commanding officer of 6/Wilts, Lieutenant Colonel George Monreal (I. C. 20), who died here several days after being wounded near Messines. The all-round views from the cemetery are excellent.

The hump-back summit of the Scherpenberg, the hill which proved to be the final straw for German hopes of 'Georgette'. (Author)

Return to the hospice and continue into Locre centre, turning right onto N375, *Kemmelbergweg,* when you get there. After a drive of 880m you will reach a junction where the N315 is signposted to Poperinge and Westoutre. This is Hyde Park Corner (not to be confused with a junction given the same name at Hill 63, near Ploegsteert) and is the furthest point of penetration of the German attack on 29 April. Ahead of you is Scherpenberg. The German attack was beaten off a few hundred metres over the fields to the right before the battle finally came to an end. How close they came to their objectives can be judged by the view that appears to your left: you can now see across much of the area between Poperinge and Ypres, where a major force of British troops were supplied, billeted and maintained. Had they been able to establish themselves on these heights, who knows what the Germans might have been capable of doing?

You will finish the tour by returning to Kemmelberg. The most straightforward way is to continue on the road until you reach the traffic roundabout at De Klijte (La Clytte), at which turn right. Continue into Kemmel and turn right where signposted for the village centre (centrum). Keep to the right of the village green and exit onto *Lokerstraat.*

An evocative tourist road sign in Kemmel. (Olivier Bayart)

You will now be driving through an area in the lee of the great hill, where reserve units sheltered below the bombardment. After 640m pull over to visit the **Lettenberg bunkers** on your right (they are also in the lee of high ground and may not be immediately visible to you: if you reach a crossroads sign, you have just over-shot the position). This site contains a chain of four restored British concrete shelters of the period (built in 1917), some of which may be entered for viewing, while others are used, for example, as a bat sanctuary.

Continue for 1180m in the direction in which you were travelling, until you reach a junction. Take the sharp left turn onto *Kemmelbergweg* and drive to the top of the hill. You will first reach a café on the left ('Au Chalet', at present) and opposite to it the **L'ossuaire national du Mont Kemmel**. Find somewhere to park; this is usually fairly simple. The ossuary is a sobering place, containing the remains of 5,294 Frenchmen who lost their lives during the battle. Only fifty-seven of them are identified. Begun in 1932, the ossuary is decorated with a central figure of the French cockerel and a number of regimental and other plaques.

The French ossuary on the heights of Kemmelberg: so many men; so few identified. (Olivier Bayart)

Walk a short but steep way up the slope of *Kemmelbergweg*, to reach the **memorial to the French troops** of 1914-1918 and specifically those

182

The impressive but somewhat hidden memorial to the French Army on the summit of Kemmelberg. (Olivier Bayart)

who fought in defence of Kemmelberg in April 1918. The impressively large, if somewhat brutal, architecture of the memorial includes a winged angel figure and an inscribed order of battle.

The rest of the summit of Kemmelberg can be seen as something of a disappointment to the battlefield tourist, these sites notwithstanding. The views are entirely obscured by trees, and there are several modern developments, such as a luxury hotel and restaurant, but a replacement of the old belvedere café still operates and provides refreshment for the many who come for today's peaceful pursuits – and that is perhaps the most fitting memorial of all.

Appendix I

Field Marshal Sir Douglas Haig's Special Order of the Day, 12 April 1918

'To all ranks of the British Army in France and Flanders. Three weeks ago to-day the enemy began his terrific attacks against us on a fifty-mile front. His objects are to separate us from the French, to take the Channel Ports, and destroy the British Army. In spite of throwing already 106 divisions into the battle, and enduring the most reckless sacrifice of human life, he has, as yet, made little progress towards his goals. We owe this to the determined fighting and self-sacrifice of our troops. Words fail me to express the admiration which I feel for the splendid resistance offered by all ranks of our Army under the most trying circumstances.

Many amongst us now are tired. To those I would say that victory will belong to the side which holds out the longest. The French Army is moving rapidly and in great force to our support. There is no other course open to us but to fight it out. Every position must be held to the last man; there must be no retirement. With our backs to the wall, and believing in the justice of our cause, each one of us must fight on to the end. The safety of our homes and the freedom of mankind depend alike upon the conduct of each one of us at this critical moment.'

Haig had issued a shorter but not dissimilar Special Order during the third day of Operation "Michael", 24 March 1918.

Appendix II

Selected Citations

Sgt S/8084 James Adamson MM, 7 Seaforth Highlanders (Motherwell). Dammstrasse, 11 April 1918. Distinguished Conduct Medal.
This non-commissioned officer led his men in a counter-attack in the face of very heavy machine-gun fire with the greatest gallantry, rallying them if they began to waver and encouraging them by his example. When the final position was reached no officers were left in his Company, of which he then took charge and consolidated the position.

BSM 16547 Charles Barnett, 218 Siege Battery, Royal Garrison Artillery (King's Cross). Dammstrasse, 10 April 1918. Distinguished Conduct Medal.
On the battery, which was in action in a forward position, receiving orders to pull out as the enemy was advancing, this NCO, under heavy gas and High Explosive bombardment, and indirect machine gun fire, displayed great courage in helping to pull out the guns, setting a wonderful example to the men, and keeping perfect control over them though a shell actually landed in the gun pit within two yards of him while he was directing the movement of the gun.

Cpl 35007 Henry Beasley, 84 Battery, Royal Field Artillery (Uxbridge). Ploegsteert Wood, 10 April 1918. Distinguished Conduct Medal.
When the enemy got close to the battery in the mist, this NCO with a party of gunners armed with rifles, held them off so that the detachments were able to destroy the guns and get away. He then joined a small party of officers and men, and fought a running fight for two hours, in the course of which they covered the withdrawal of a heavy howitzer battery.

Acting Company Sergeant Major WR/268321 Edward Beavis, 14 Light Railway Company, Royal Engineers (Southampton). Kemmelberg, 17 April 1918. Distinguished Conduct Medal.
On several occasions, in spite of hostile shelling of a most intense description, he brought up trains to advanced Royal Army Medical Corps stretcher bearer posts, and took away large numbers of British and French wounded, who could not be evacuated by road on account of the heavy shelling. The railway track was frequently blown up by shell fire, but this

gallant NCO immediately had the gaps repaired. The assistance he rendered to the medical services was invaluable, and his cheerful and unremitting devotion to duty was most marked.

Sous-Lieutenant (Réserve) Maurice-Moïse Chazel, 3 Machine Gun Company, 99 Régiment d'Infanterie. Kemmelberg, 17 April 1918. Légion d'Honneur.
A young officer of courage and remarkable sang-froid, always ready for the most perilous missions. Distinguished in all of the actions in which he took part with the regiment. In spite of the intense bombing to which Kemmelberg was subjected, on which his company was located, he did not hesitate to go forward to reconnoitre the crest where his section was to be positioned. He was gravely wounded during his mission.

Lance Sergeant 24872 Herbert Conroy, 1/6 Duke of Wellington's (West Riding Regiment) (Bradford). Kemmel, 26 April 1918. Distinguished Conduct Medal.
When one of the officers of his company was reported to be missing, he immediately went out with a small patrol to search for him, penetrating through the enemy's positions and searching the ground in rear of them. The next morning, he followed up the attack of another battalion, and continued his search beyond the positions taken up by the attacking battalion, going close up to the enemy's line in daylight. On a subsequent occasion, when his company were subjected to a bombardment of unusual intensity, he took command of his platoon when all the other NCOs had become casualties. He rescued three men who had been buried by a shell explosion, and he set a very fine example of courage and energy, going about regardless of danger, organising and encouraging the men.

Private 40458 Frank Cross MM, 75 Field Ambulance, Royal Army Medical Corps (Paddington). Petit Munque Farm near Ploegsteert, 11 April 1918. Distinguished Conduct Medal.
For conspicuous gallantry and devotion to duty with a party of stretcher bearers during an enemy attack. When two bearers were hit he crawled out from behind a farmhouse and carried in one. Then, accompanied by a Sergeant of the Field Ambulance, he went out to bring in the other bearer, but the Sergeant was hit. He dragged in the second bearer and went out a third time and helped the Sergeant to cover. His conduct throughout was magnificent.

Sergeant 330271 James Diamond, 1/9 Battalion, Highland Light Infantry (Glasgow). Near Neuve Eglise, 13 April 1918. Distinguished Conduct Medal.

When the enemy had got through the front line he went out with details from battalion headquarters and drove them back, accounting for at least twenty himself with a Lewis gun. Throughout he set an example of the utmost coolness, and was always to the fore in bringing up his Lewis guns to any threatened part of the line.

Lieutenant Henry Fowler MC, Royal Engineers (Tottenham). Pont de Nieppe bridge, 10 April 1918. Bar to Military Cross.

After the demolition of a bridge over a river, it was discovered that four men were struggling in the water on the enemy side. He immediately procured some planks and part of a demolished bridge which had floated down and successfully effected the rescue of these men on his own initiative under continuous enemy rifle fire.

Bombardier 26939 Edward Hards, 6 Siege Battery, Royal Garrison Artillery (Worthing). Near Dranoutre, 15 April 1918. Distinguished Conduct Medal.

This NCO, in charge of the advanced wagon lines, has ably dealt with difficult situations. On no less than five occasions he has brought up the gun teams and removed the guns under intense fire. On one occasion, a complete gun team being knocked out, he reorganised the teams and brought away all the guns and wagons under heavy fire. His coolness and example has kept the drivers up to a high standard.

Lieutenant Frank Forbes Higginson, 109 Railway Company, Royal Engineers. Location uncertain; unit headquartered at St Hubertushoek, 11 April 1918. Military Cross.

By his gallant conduct and resource he succeeded in safely extricating a 12-inch howitzer [of 359 Siege Battery, Royal Garrison Artillery] and locomotive, with several trucks of ammunition, under heavy shell fire. On this and other occasions he has shown the greatest energy and initiative, setting an inspiring example to all ranks.

Second Lieutenant John Illingworth, 1/6 Battalion, West Yorkshire Regiment attached to 49 Divisional Traffic Control. Mont Noir, 17 April 1918. Military Cross.

For conspicuous gallantry and devotion to duty. During an exceedingly heavy shelling a number of men of a labour company were wounded. With great coolness he organised some of his men and succeeded in bringing eighteen wounded men under cover, where he dressed and bandaged them. When in charge of straggler and traffic posts, he continually visited his posts under heavy shell fire, and by his example gave his men confidence to carry out their duty under most trying circumstances. [John Illingworth was killed by a shell on 3 June 1918 and is buried at Hagle Dump Cemetery, near Brandhoek.]

Second Lieutenant George Leighton, 4 Battalion, South African Infantry (Transvaal Scottish). Messines, 10 April 1918. Military Cross.
For conspicuous gallantry and devotion to duty. At a critical period, when the other officers of his company had become casualties, he took command of all the units in the vicinity, as well as of his own, and established a strong defensive position at a time when the enemy attack was imminent. He moved about under very heavy fire, from shell hole to shell hole, until he had completed his dispositions; and his courage and fearless devotion to duty were examples to all those under him, re-establishing their steadfastness and enabling him to control men who were quite strangers to him at a moment when a firm resistance was of the utmost value.

Sergeant 19244 Arthur Mogg, 4 Battalion Worcestershire Regiment (Bromsgrove). Steenwerck Station, 11 April 1918. Distinguished Conduct Medal.
An advanced post was being heavily trench mortared, and the enemy was attempting to capture it. Notwithstanding the heavy shelling he took over a Lewis gun and did exceptionally good work with it, and, in spite of a wound, refused to leave the gun until the enemy had withdrawn.

Acting Corporal 31285 Victor Pace MM, 28 Field Ambulance, Royal Army Medical Corps (Leytonstone). Vierstraat, 25 April 1918. Distinguished Conduct Medal.
The officer in charge of the [stretcher] bearers having been wounded, this NCO volunteered to go and find out why no wounded were coming in from a regimental aid post. He found that one medical officer had been taken prisoner, and the other had moved farther back, so, though exposed to fire of all sorts, he personally organised and carried out the evacuation of the wounded from the front line.

Private 43849 George Poole, 9 Battalion, Machine Gun Corps (Cambridge Heath). Near Hollebeke, 11 April 1918. Distinguished Conduct Medal.
This man volunteered to accompany some bombers to reconnoitre

pillboxes which had been rushed by the enemy the previous day and in which three machine guns had been left. He retrieved one of the guns under heavy fire and was severely wounded by a sniper, but hung on to the gun and crawled back with it until he collapsed and was carried in.

Private M/3013209 Benjamin Sermon, Army Service Corps (Mechanical Transport), attached to 101 Field Ambulance, Royal Army Medical Corps (Bermondsey). Near Neuve Eglise, 11 April 1918. Distinguished Conduct Medal.
Without being asked, he drove his car through the enemy outposts and evacuated all the wounded from an aid post, returning under heavy fire. He was on duty for 48 hours, and cleared wounded in full view of the enemy. He did fine service.

Company Sergeant Major 16999 George Sutton, 18 Battalion, King's (Liverpool Regiment) (Walton, Liverpool). Near Voormezele, 29 April 1918. Distinguished Conduct Medal.
During a violent attack by the enemy, a party of about twenty succeeded in entering one of the advanced posts. This Warrant Officer attacked them, single-handed, with bombs, killing and wounding a number and recapturing the post. The enemy had penetrated at a most important point, and, had he been given time to establish himself, it would have taken a large force to eject him.

Soldat (Réserve) 6792 Joseph Vagneux, 5 Company, 414 Régiment d'Infanterie. Near Kemmelberg, 29 April 1918. Médaille Militaire.
An excellent soldier, having always valiantly accomplished his duty. Seriously wounded at his post while helping to repel an enemy attack. Left hand amputated.

Second Lieutenant John Woolley, 4 Battalion, South Staffordshire Regiment. Kemmel, 26 April 1918. Military Cross.
For conspicuous gallantry and devotion to duty during an attack. When the right flank of the battalion was held up by enemy machine guns hidden in a farm, he rushed forward with a small party, surrounded the farm and captured it, killing most of the garrison and taking eleven prisoners and two machine guns. His prompt action and great gallantry allowed the attack, which would otherwise have been held up, to proceed according to programme.

Appendix III

The Phases of the Battles of the Lys
9th April – 29th April 1918

As defined by the British Battles Nomenclature Committee, which published their report in 1922. The battles shown in italics took place wholly within the geographic area of the *Objective Ypres* volume.

- The Battle of Estaires, 9 – 11 April 1918
- *The Battle of Messines, 10 – 11 April 1918*
- The Battle of Hazebrouck, 12 – 15 April 1918
- *The Battle of Bailleul, 13 – 15 April 1918*
- *The First Battle of Kemmel, 17 – 19 April 1918*
- The Battle of Béthune, 18 April 1918
- *The Second Battle of Kemmel, 25 – 26 April 1918*
- *The Battle of the Scherpenberg, 29 April 1918.*

Acknowledgements

I have been most fortunate to receive support and advice from a wide range of organisations and individuals when carrying out the research for this book.

Most of the narrative detail is drawn from operational records held in the WO95 (war diaries) series at the National Archives in Kew, London, and from their equivalents at the Australian War Memorial; from the records of officers held in the WO339 and WO374 collections; from the service records of other ranks which are held by the National Archives but now accessible online via Ancestry and Findmypast; from the prisoner of war records held by the International Committee of the Red Cross; and from private memoirs and papers held at the Imperial War Museum. The latter's library has also been an excellent source of published German regimental and unit histories. My own library of books and collections of various documents gathered over the years has also been plundered.

All reasonable efforts have been made in order to identify copyright owners where this was initially unknown, particularly of photographs. Wherever possible, photographs that are stated to be in the public domain have been used. Readers attention is drawn to the superb collections of photographs of the battle at the Imperial War Museum, freely available to see at their website but unfortunately priced too highly to be viable for inclusion in a publication such as this.

I have been helped in a hundred small ways in the production of this book, not least by series editor Nigel Cave, but I also wish to mention the only other person who has ever seemed particularly interested in this battle, my friend Phil Tomaselli, who wrote the Battleground Europe volume covering the southern part of the action, *The Battle of the Lys 1918: Givenchy and the River Lawe*. I seem to follow him around the area, always seeing his signature in the cemetery registers. I should also specifically like to thank Jack Sheldon, historian of the German Army, whose knowledge and access to its histories is surely unsurpassed; Brett Butterworth for his wonderful collection of photographs of German soldiers; Genevra Charsley and Jacques Ryckebosch; Sarah Yukich (Kerry Stokes Collection) and Dean Mighell for the use of the photograph of 'Ted' Falloon from the Thuillier Collection; Suzanne Foster, the Winchester College archivist for the use of the photograph of Laurence Booth; and finally my son Lawrence, for spending hours photographing officers' records, and my wife Geraldine for her endless patience!

Any errors found within the text of the book are wholly mine.

Selective Bibliography

There are very few works that cover the whole battle.

The British Official History, "History of the Great War based on official documents – Military Operations France and Belgium 1918, March-April: continuation of the German offensive" by Sir James Edmonds (London: Macmillan, 1937) is the most comprehensive and a remarkably readable volume.

My own "The Battle for Flanders: German defeat on the Lys, 1918" (Barnsley: Pen & Sword Military, 2011) is the only modern study that I have ever been able to find.

I understand that a new study by Andrew Rawson, part of a series of works covering the phases of the Great War, is to be published by Pen & Sword Military around the same time as this book.

There are some other very good works that provide information on particular aspects of the battle. The published histories of the various divisions and regiments vary in depth and quality, but provide useful background, and are always worth consulting. In addition to those, I would recommend the following as a "starting list":

British
Griffith, Paddy (ed.) British fighting methods in the Great War (London: Frank Cass, 1996)
Griffith, Paddy. Battle tactics of the Western Front (London: Yale University Press, 1994)
Hankey, Lord. The Supreme Command 1914-1918, Volume 2 (London: George Allen and Unwin, 1961)
Jones, H. A. History of the Great War based on official documents by direction of the Historical Section of the Committee of Imperial Defence. The War in the Air: being the story of the part played in the Great War by the Royal Air Force. Vol. IV (Oxford: Clarendon Press, 1934)
Zabecki, David T. The German offensives 1918: a case study on the operational level of war (Abingdon: Routledge, 2006)

French
France, Etat-major des armées, Service historique. Les armées françaises dans la Grande Guerre, Tome VI. (French Official History)

Mott, Colonel T. Bentley (transl.) The memoirs of Marshal Foch (London; William Heinemann, 1931)

Rouquerol, General J. Le Kemmel, 1918 (Paris: Payot, 1936)

German

Goes, Gustav. Kemmel - Sturm und Sterben um einen Berg (Berlin, Tradition Wilhelm Kolk, 1932)

Kabish, Ernest. Um Lys und Kemmel (Berlin: Vorhut-Verlag, 1936)

Kuhl, Hermann von. Der deutsche Generalstab in Vorbereitung und Durchfuhrung des Weltkrieges (Berlin: Deutsche Verlag, 1920)

Ludendorff, Erich. My war memories 1914-1918, Volume 2 (London: Hutchinson & Co, 1919)

Ludendorff, Erich. The nation at war (London: Hutchinson & Co, 1936)

Reichsarchiv Der Weltkrieg 1914–1918: Die militarischen Operationen zu Lande: Vierzehnter Band: Die Kriegführung an der Westfront im Jahre 1918 (Berlin: E. S. Mittler und Sohn, 1944).

Index

194

Torreken, 55, 59, 153
Underhill, 34, 36
Westhof, 86, 164
Fausset-Crivelli, Lt L., 101
Finch, Lt Col L., 33
Foch, Marshal F., 15–16, 98–9, 107
French Armies
DAN, 107
Corps
II Cavalry, 98–9, 108
Divisions
2 Cavalry, 99
3 Cavalry, 99
6 Cavalry, 99
28, 93, 97, 99–101, 105, 108
34, 108
39, 108, 122–3, 127
133, 98, 108
154, 108, 124, 127, 180
Regiments
22, 100
30, 108, 111–12, 114
99, 105
154, 127
156, 127–8
413, 112
416, 110, 112–13
Freyberg, Brig Gen B., 41

Garfield, Pte J., 157
Garrett, 2/Lt A., 106
Garthwaite, Maj A., 55
Gent, CSM J., 24
German Armies
Groups
Rupprecht's, 6, 106
Armies
Fourth, 6, 8, 12, 14–15, 17, 19–
20, 79, 85, 92, 102–103, 106,
115, 120, 125, 131, 170
Sixth, 6, 8, 13–14, 17, 19, 79,
85, 92, 107, 170

Corps
Guard, 106
II Bavarian, 72
X Reserve, 15, 72, 108
XVIII, 15, 21, 44, 108
Divisions
Alpine Corps, 85, 108, 111–12,
115, 123, 127, 179
1st Bavarian, 15
4th Bavarian, 108, 112, 124,
127, 144, 180
7th, 57, 59, 96, 108, 119, 125
10th Ersatz, 66, 93
11th Bavarian, 72, 85, 165
11th Reserve, 85, 165
13th Reserve, 107–108, 118,
125
17th, 15
17th Reserve, 15, 32, 44, 59,
151, 156
19th Reserve, 107–108, 118–
19, 125
22nd Reserve, 15, 108
31st, 15, 21, 31–2, 145
32nd, 13, 85, 93, 165
36th, 15
36th Reserve, 77
38th, 67, 104
49th Reserve, 15, 21, 44
56th, 108, 112, 118
117th, 72, 85, 87, 93, 165
214th, 15, 21, 72, 141
233rd, 107
Regiments
Bavarian Leib, 112–13, 115,
127
1 Bavarian Jäger, 112, 115
2 Bavarian Jäger, 112–14
39, 125
70, 31, 145
71, 104
73 Reserve, 119

200

Huns Walk, 156
Hyde Park, 127–8, 181
Hyde Park Corner, 34, 145
Kellow Crossing, 172
In der Kruisstraat Cabaret, 51, 63
Junction Buildings, 45, 53
Keersebrom, 87–8, 104
Kingsway, 108
Kortepyp Cabaret, 71, 163–4
Lancashire Cottage, 139
Leinster Road, 70, 72, 74, 144, 162
Lettenberg bunkers, 182
Locre Hospice, 180
Louis Windmill, 102
Maison '1875', 27
Manchester Post, 39, 171
Manchester Street, 46
Mendinghem, 42
Milky Way, 118
Motor Car Corner, 141
Mud Lane, 145
Nicholson's Avenue, 25
North House, 50, 96–8, 116, 118, 154
Oak Trench, 150
Oak Support, 57–8, 150
Oak Switch, 150
Papot Mill, 173
Parret Camp, 96
Peckham Crater, 97–8
Pick House, 47, 49–51, 53, 59, 61, 155
Pompier, 128
Quarry Road, 144
Railway Switch, 24, 141
Red Lodge, 36, 145
Reserve Avenue, 25, 141
Seddon Camp, 57
Spanbroekmolen, 50, 92–3, 96–7, 100, 157–8

Spoil Bank, 120, 125, 149
Staenyzer Cabaret crossroads, 60, 95, 152–3, 155
Stampkotmolen, 78
Steenwerck Station, 41, 63, 65, 170, 172–3
Suicide Road, 155
Thornton Road, 85
Le Touquet Station, 24, 140–1
La Trompe Cabaret, 70, 74, 78, 161–2
Ultimo Avenue, 31
Ultimo Crater, 33, 146
Vleugelhoek, 124
Watchful Post, 32
Waterloo Road, 76, 164
Wigan Post, 39
White Chateau, 57–8, 150
Wytschaete Hospice, 153–4
York House, 118
Zambuk Track, 33
Tudor, Maj Gen H., 15
Turner, 2/Lt F., 177

Umfreville, Lt Col R., 51

Vercoe, Cpl F., 144

Wait, Capt G., 34
Walker, 2/Lt A., 32
Wilhelm, Crown Prince, 4
William, Maj H., 56
Wilson, Gen Sir H., 11, 102
Woods
　Bayernwald, 154
　Bois Confluent, 119
　Bois de la Hutte, 137
　Bois Quarante, 118–19
　Delville, 51
　Denys, 56, 58–60, 151
　Grand Bois, 58, 97, 118, 154, 158